The
SHOULDING

A Story of Resilience and Hope

By Roberta Brown

PAGE PUBLISHING, INC.
New York, NY

First originally published by Page Publishing, Inc. 2016

ISBN 978-1-68348-025-9 (pbk)
ISBN 978-1-68348-026-6 (digital)

Printed in the United States of America

DEDICATION

To my best friend Tricia: You are the valve to my pressure cooker. You love me for who I am with no judgment whatsoever. How lucky I am to have met you that day in tenth-grade art class! My life wouldn't be the same without you. I love you tons and bunches, bigger than the universe!

——ACKNOWLEDGMENTS——

I would like to thank the following people for their unconditional love and support. I am grateful for each and every one of you.

Achirai, Ann, Anita, Aunt Marilyan, Beth, Charlene, Cousin Shellie, Cynthia, Elaine, Glenda, Jackie, Jenny, Karen, Kurt, Kym, Layne, Leah B., Lynn F., Michael, Michael R., Nancy G., Philip, Roxanne, Sharon, Sharon R., Sim, Soma, Soultar, Tricia, Vern, Vonne, Wendy.

I feel fortunate that I've surrounded myself with the right people...finally!

# FOREWORD

I have been a psychologist since the early seventies and have worked with a rather large number of clients with anxiety disorders, obsessive-compulsive disorder, panic, and agoraphobia. Many of my patients I've worked with for short to moderate lengths of time. I've worked with and have dealt with the author's complications and issues from her young adulthood on.

I originally saw Roberta in 1984 at a clinic in Minneapolis, and given her complications, particularly with men, it seemed wise to have her work with a female therapist. Years later, we mutually agreed to work together, and have on and off for thirty-one years.

This book is her effort to have a healthy perspective on her life, its complications and its triumphs.

I know she put her heart and soul into this effort at not being "done in" by a difficult childhood. I would see this as one person's successful effort in overcoming the complications of a challenging childhood.

It has been a satisfying experience to see her evolve and develop into a healthy, psychologically functioning woman, which is obviously due more to her efforts than mine.

She is the client that really has worked harder than her therapist in pulling her life together. It gives me satisfaction that I played some role in her success.

[Name withheld], PhD

——— INTRODUCTION ———

SHOULD [shood]:

1. Past tense of shall
2. Used to express obligation or duty
3. Used to express probability or expectation
4. Used to moderate the directness or bluntness of a statement: "I should think he would want to go."

SHOULDING [shood-ing]:

My definition:

After inflicting major guilt on yourself, doing what you think would be expected of you, even if it's not appreciated. This is more than a sense of duty, making it a way of life almost to the distraction of everything else, including one's own well-being.

---————— CHAPTER 1 ——————---

Shoulding on Yourself

The irony is not lost on me that I'm starting to write this on the one-year anniversary of my father's death. In Judaism the one-year anniversary is called a Yahrzeit. This is when, as a Jew, we end our period of mourning and commemorate the day by reciting the Mourner's Kaddish, usually as service at the synagogue. I can honestly say I have been struggling with whether I wanted to attend this service and honor my father at all. My sense of all "SHOULD" is a strong one. I have lived my life with "SHOULDING" and disregarding my true feelings. This memoir I'm embarking on is this story of my journey to mental and emotional health. It certainly has been a long, tough road.

I was born in Minneapolis December of 1958, twelve years after my only sibling. I was told I was "the most wanted baby in America." My understanding is that there were several miscarriages, and my parents were told they probably couldn't have another child. But years later "I took." I was stubborn even then.

I don't have a lot of recollection of my really early years. I don't know if anyone does. I do remember a lot of yelling. My parents yelling at each other, and then yelling at my sister and me. I also remember some family trips. We went to Chicago to visit my grandparents, my aunt and uncle, and cousins. We went to California to vacation and visit relatives. In writing it down it all seems a bit benign. We had chalk portraits done at Disneyland. My sister laughed as she was making me sick on the Teacup Ride. The sicker I got, the harder she laughed. The rest are just memories through pictures.

We took fishing trips up north to Brainerd, Gull Lake, and Eshquaguma. I swam, I skied, I played tennis. I was the closest thing to a jock my dad would have. He always wanted boys, but no such luck. That didn't stop him from letting us know how we fell short in that department. I know that writing my story is going to open up a lot of pain for me, but I'm hoping it will be a healing, cathartic experience.

How do we know that we are living in a "normal" family? Who defines "normal?" As I said, growing up there was a lot of yelling, a lot of fighting. As time went on, fighting became emotional and physical abuse from my father—my mother's role in this I didn't really realize until I was fifty-one.

Time to take a deep, cleansing breath…

My really early memories of abuse were being slapped in the face, in the head, and spanked on my behind. I only recall a specific spanking when I was seven or eight after accidentally breaking a floodlight at a neighbor's pond. I was so afraid to own up to it, and when I did, I was spanked and told I would have to pay for the floodlight and apologize to the neighbors. I was grounded as well. Pretty harsh for an accident. That was a theme in our house.

Early on I was labeled as "stupid, careless, and lazy." I don't know why. I was never any of those things. But that was a constant. I accidentally broke a dish from a set of Royal Doulton china my parents brought back from England. All hell broke loose. Not only was I stupid, careless, and lazy, I was going to pay for being all of those things. I had to order a replacement dish and go pay for it. Mind you, this was not like a Greek wedding where people break plates on purpose, it was an accident. Oh, I was grounded after that too. I started becoming afraid to touch any material thing that belonged to my parents.

When I was sixteen, my parents went on vacation and left me alone for the first time. As any sixteen-year-old I planned to have a party. I called this the "don't break the yellow lamp" party. Only my best friend came. Who would come to a party that would be focused on not breaking anything?

The night before they came back, I loaded the dishwasher to make sure everything would be clean and put away when they got back. In the morning, I unloaded the clean dishes and put everything away. I went and picked them up at the airport and brought them home. That night my dad opened up a little cupboard under the counter in the kitchen. Out fell a white Corningware dish and broke into two pieces. I froze! I knew what was going to happen. But how could it? I made sure everything was clean and put away. This was just exactly what I was trying to avoid. The screaming and belittling started. "How could you be so stupid, careless, and lazy? You're going to go buy us a new one." I don't think he hit me that time, but the name calling was enough, too much in fact. I realized I was afraid. Afraid of everything, all the time.

I grew up on a cul-de-sac in a beautiful part of town. We had a nice house. Nothing too big or fancy. There was a big backyard that was bordered by some woods. It was the only house I lived in growing up. Pretty idyllic, or so it seemed. We didn't want for material things. In fact, material things seemed really important to my parents. We had the latest TV, radios, stereos. My dad loved buying gadgets. My mom liked things "just so." Everything in its place. The problem was everything seemed to be "surfacy." A family in a nice house, in a nice neighborhood, who belonged to a synagogue, were members of a golf club, and who went on vacations together. So why didn't anyone get along? My parents fought or belittled each other a good percentage of the time. My sister and I didn't get along. She spent a lot of time tormenting me. I spent a lot of time trying to knit a family together. I wanted my parents and my sister to love me so badly. Well, badly is what I got.

I didn't know it then, but after much therapy, I realized I was raised by a family of narcissists. The problem, I wasn't one. There was a lot of attention given to the way things looked. But more than that, there was a lot of self-involvement and self-centeredness by my parents and my sister. It was nothing I understood as a small child. I think that was where I got the notion that things seemed "surfacy," maybe even disingenuous.

CHAPTER 2

OCD, PTSD
and Other Disorders

PTSD—posttraumatic stress disorder. That happens to war veterans, right? I remember hearing about PTSD in association with the Vietnam War. Never in a million years did I think PTSD would be a big part of my life. PTSD for me rears its ugly head in many different ways. Sometimes I split right out of my body and view things from above where the things are happening to me. Sometimes it's ringing in my ears; sometimes it's no ringing at all. Sometimes I go blank and sit as time passes. Sometimes I go blank, continue doing tasks, "come to," and it's been several hours. Things are put away, laundry is done, drawers and closets organized, and I have no recollection. If I have to choose one, the blanking out and getting stuff done would be my preference, although the "losing time" part doesn't sit too well with me. It has never happened while I'm driving myself around. I know that if something has got me really upset, I would call my best friend and have her talk to me to keep me centered. Other PTSD symptoms would be uncontrollable shaking and crying and/or not being able to sleep. It all depends on what the trigger is.

My first PTSD incident I remember clearly was when I was walking around outside when I was five. I don't know if my parents and I were planning on going somewhere, but I remember I had on a pink dress with the bow in the back. I walked over to my neighbor's house across the street. We were standing by their willow tree. The next thing I knew, one of the girls I was friends with, her cousin, and a couple boys from the neighborhood knocked me down. I heard someone yell, "strip her." I didn't even know what that meant. I realized they were trying to pull my dress off. I was suddenly watching everything from above in the willow tree. It was very confusing. First of all, how could I watch this from up there? Secondly, why were they doing that? That's all I remember. I hadn't done anything to them. I SHOULD have been safe to walk around in my neighborhood where I knew everyone. It just added more fuel to my notion of being scared of everything all of the time.

One of the more unusual PTSD events I had was when I was married. My mother was in the hospital at the University of Minnesota yet again. I had been to the hospital to visit her on my own many times over the years. I had never had a problem getting there and back. But this time would be different. My then husband was driving his brown Mercury Sable, and I was the passenger. We got out to the hospital just fine. We visited for a couple of hours. We were on our way back to the car, and I asked him not to take the highway because I didn't want to get stuck in traffic. I told him I was nervous and upset, and it would make it easier on me if we took a different way home. He said sure. We were on our way home, and the next thing I knew he was getting on the ramp to the highway. I begged him not to. There was traffic! I began to cry. I closed my eyes. When I opened them his car looked like the inside of my mother's blue 1974 Buick LeSabre. It was exactly what I saw when my mother was telling me I wouldn't be dancing with the Minnesota Dance Theater. How could this be? That was twenty years before. But the interior of my then-husband's car looked just like the blue Buick, not the brown Sable we were riding in. I was panicked! What was happening? Then I realized it must be some PTSD reaction to not being in control of my destiny or destination. I can only remember that kind of PTSD event happening that one time.

I have always had a certain amount of anxiety for as long as I remember. I knew as a little girl, going to school was hard. My mom would walk me to the bus stop, and I would cry when I had to get on the bus. Whether that was separation anxiety or fear of what unknown thing was going to happen at school, I was not sure. But again, I was afraid of everything all of the time.

There have been some more recent out-of-body PTSD events. I think it was three years ago at another "lovely," dysfunctional Thanksgiving dinner at my sister's. Things had gone pretty smoothly. No fighting, not much belittling, probably because my sister had invited some friends of hers to join us. So I would say best behavior was being displayed. I was all for it! As usual, after dinner, I was clearing plates and cleaning up. I went back to the table to take a plate from my niece, and she and my dad were in some kind of deep discussion. As I walked up I heard my dad say to her, "Maybe I was too hard on my kids." Out of my body I went. I was up and to the right of myself, watching. Their conversation continued. I couldn't hear what was being said, but I could see my niece trying to make eye contact with me. When she did finally make eye contact, I came back. It really was only a matter of seconds. No one knew. She handed me her plate and life went on.

One of the more lengthy and dramatic PTSD events occurred two years ago. My niece and nephew were in from out of town. We were supposed to meet up at my dad and stepmother's condo. I had already decided it was best for me not to stay for dinner. I had made other plans to be with my then-boyfriend. I had been realizing that my "family" was toxic at best. When I arrived the only other people there were Dad and his wife. I started putting appetizers on a plate while I stood in their kitchen. Dad and his wife started fighting. It started with his wife making some snippy remarks about my dad. He started to make snide remarks back. I could feel myself tensing up. They were fighting in the doorway, the only way out of the kitchen. I had my back to them. I kept saying soothing things to myself. I turned around and there was my ninety-two-year-old father with his

16

wife backed up against the wall, her walker between them. He had his fists up and his shoulders flinching forward at her. He had that look I was all too familiar with. My mind started racing. What do I do? SHOULD I step in and take the punch for her? SHOULD I knock him down? I couldn't speak or scream out. My answer to both questions, no I SHOULDN'T. I was managing to stay in my body. But I was trapped in the kitchen. I was trying to reason everything out. No, I would not take a punch for her. I had taken too many of my own. No, I would not knock him down. He could break a hip, and more importantly, I could be charged with elder abuse. It's amazing how many things race through your mind when feeling threatened. His fists were still up when my sister walked in and said to him, "Why are you yelling?" Before she could come around the corner, Dad's fists were down and his wife was using her walker to move forward. I on the other hand got the hell out of the kitchen. As crazy as that scene seems, the craziest thing was sitting down at the dining room table as if nothing had happened. Of course my niece and nephew hadn't heard anything, so they were none the wiser. I was able to sit there for about fifteen minutes and then got up and said good-bye. I walked out the door, walked down the long hallway and out to the front of the building. I noticed my breathing was off. Sort of fast, but not like hyperventilating. I got in my car, and I started to gasp for air. I tried to talk to myself about deep-cleansing breaths. I called my best friend. As soon as I heard her voice, I lost it. I was crying so hard. I begged her to talk to me while I drove myself back home. She told me to catch my breath before I started to drive. As soon as I was calm, I told her what happened. She said, "What the fuck is wrong with your dad?" She talked to me until I got upstairs to my apartment. I was much calmer. I told her I was OK and would call her later. My then-boyfriend arrived not knowing what had happened. We ended up going out to dinner, but I couldn't stop shaking. I could see my hair shaking. He dropped me off and asked me if I wanted him to stay. I said no, I was OK. I spent the majority of the evening sitting in the dark, shaking. When I went to bed I thought that sleep would be easy. No such luck. Everything that happened at Dad's kept playing back like a looped movie. I found myself shaking and cold. I couldn't stop crying. I never did get any sleep that night. I can tell you I didn't feel safe again around my "family." It didn't matter how much I did with and for them, I was never safe and never secure in knowing any of them had my back in any way. Out of all the PTSD episodes, the uncontrollable shaking, crying, and rerunning it like a movie would be my least favorite. It felt like going into shock. Maybe that's what it truly was.

I don't think I've even had a small PTSD event since May of 2013. That time I was talking to my favorite aunt on the phone, and she started telling me something unflattering that my stepmother had told her about me. Not only was it not nice, but it was untrue. What was it? I don't remember. All I know for sure, I talked a little longer to my aunt and hung up the phone. The next thing I knew, it was two hours later. I popped back into my body and saw I had organized a bunch of closets and drawers. That's how I prefer my PTSD to be, productive. Whatever my aunt told me must've been upsetting. Besides organizing my things, the other good thing that came out of it was I realized I didn't have to have a relationship with my stepmother anymore. Dad was dead, and I owed her nothing. But there will be more about that later. Maybe in its own way, PTSD is productive, maybe with enough therapy…

OCD —obsessive compulsive disorder. That's when people wash their hands a lot, right? Yes, but it's so much more. For me, OCD started with counting. I didn't know it at the time, but I would count how many steps it took me to get from the bus stop to my house when I was in school. I thought it was a fun game I played. But it seemed to me there was a quieter more subtle count going on often. It wasn't until my twenties when I had full-blown anxiety that the OCD became a serious problem. There was incessant counting, washing hands, constant cleaning, and organizing. Certain numbers were problematic, mostly multiples of six. OCD doesn't make sense. While the things that trigger us to do what we do are interesting if you're reading about it as a case study, living it is a much different thing. For me, any thoughts that made me anxious started me counting. When I started to talk to my therapist about it, he said that it had a name, intrusive thinking. For some reason it helped me to know it had a name. That meant, at least to me, that I didn't think of it, and I probably wasn't crazy or alone. Intrusive thinking for me meant that I was having inexplicable strange thoughts.

One very clear memory was when I was married. I thought I was going to take a knife and plunge it into my upper thigh. The logical side of me wondered why I would think something like that. I had no reason or motivation to do that. Where does a thought like that come from? The "afraid of everything all the time" side of me thought that I should hide all the knives. I would also know where they were. Explaining that makes it seem funny somehow. Needless to say, I never plunged a knife into my thigh or any other part of myself…ever. I had to learn to let those thoughts come and just as easily let them go. There weren't a lot of thoughts like that, but enough to make me worry if I was as sick as my family had always told me I was. My therapist assured me that if I just "practiced" letting the thoughts go, they would go. He was right. I'm a pretty organized person, so OCD wasn't my biggest problem. Before I would leave my apartment, I would unplug things like the toaster oven and coffeepot every time. I still do that, but it doesn't feel like a "have to do" thing. Now I don't do it every time I go somewhere. I can even proudly say my work desk is not perfectly organized, and there are a couple piles of papers I need to go through. Good for me! How normal!

Back in the throes of my OCD, I did wash my hands until they were raw. I don't do that anymore. But if you need wet wipes, I do have some in my purse.

Agoraphobia—translated means fear of the marketplace. For me that was a serious problem. When I was twenty-three, I had just been transferred to a store a little further away than I was used to driving. I had been a manager of a kiosk in a north suburb of the Twin Cities. I was on my way to work, and I became frightened. Nothing I could put my finger on. So I exited the highway and pulled over. I gave myself a pep talk, and pretty soon I was back on the highway. I was nearing the mall when traffic came to a total standstill. There were police cars and fire trucks. I think one of the firemen was walking down the traffic line letting us know what was happening. There was a live power line down on the highway. No one was going anywhere until the wire was picked up. I started to hyperventilate and sweat. I looked left and right. There was no getting around the cars. There was no way to drive across the grass. We were all stuck. I was stuck. And no cell phones back then. I could feel my mounting panic. I was sure I was having a heart attack. I was catastrophizing. I felt sick; I felt I might die right there. I think we sat for almost an hour. Once I got to the store, I couldn't work. I had someone drive me home. I never went back. I couldn't face possibly getting stuck in traffic again. My ability to go anywhere started to dwindle. That's when I went for a mental health intake interview. That's where I met my current therapist. He was the intake doctor. He evaluated me, and then I started seeing a wonderful woman therapist. A lot was going on in my life. I was making a lot of bad choices about things that were causing my full-blown anxiety, which eventually turned into agoraphobia. I did not leave my house by myself for two years. If someone would take me to the grocery store, they had to stay right next to me. Those trips would be short and disorienting. It was hard for me to go get my mail and to go to the laundry room. I had therapy assistants who would help me. I went on Social Security disability so that I could pay my rent. I knew I had to work really hard to get better.

And so the work began. First, I had to learn about agoraphobia. I read Hope and Help for Your Nerves by Claire Weekes. There was a lot of explanation. It would have been interesting reading about it as a case study; living it, not so much. She wrote about different techniques to deal with the anxiety and panic. "Floating through" was one of them. You were supposed to imagine yourself floating away from the anxiety. It worked, but only to a point. Most agoraphobics feel their home is their safe place. But what happens if your panic and anxiety are 24-7? I remember feeling like I had to run away. But to where? I didn't think I had the ability to leave my apartment. I think that's called a double bind. So with me afraid of everything all of the time, history, it just doubled or tripled that feeling. In those two years that I spent in my apartment, I don't remember a lot. I just remember how it felt. How frightening it all was. The first therapist I worked with was great. She suggested trying antianxiety medication. That scared me too. We talked about pros and cons of each drug.

Nardil was one that I remember I wouldn't take because I wouldn't be able to eat aged cheese. No one messes with my cheese. Prozac was another drug we talked about. I'm pretty sure that's when Del Shannon's wife was on the Phil Donahue show saying that Prozac had caused Del to commit suicide. So that was out. The only thing I agreed to was an as-needed prescription for Ativan. I wanted to power through. Often I would wake up in the middle of the night having a panic attack. I would run to the window, open it, and breathe in all the fresh air I could. Then I would calm down and try to go back to sleep. When I couldn't, I would take a quarter of an Ativan. If I took a small amount I wouldn't feel so loopy. What I've learned over the years is that anxiety disorders have a lot to do with the loss of confidence in your own thinking processes. Always second guessing why you're thinking what you're thinking. Coupled with my upbringing, in retrospect, it was not so surprising that I suffered from all these anxiety-related disorders. An interesting caveat, as I was starting to get better and becoming more mobile, that was when both of my parents admitted they both had panic disorders in their pasts. They told me about some of their anxiety events, then in the same breath told me that I wasn't having anxiety the "right way" because I was letting it bother me too much.

Sound like another "giving and taking away" thing? So this led me to do some research. Was there a genetic component to anxiety disorders? And if there was, because both my parents had it, wouldn't that mean I got a double genetic whammy? And does it matter? We're all individuals and handle things how we handle them. Many years later my sister admitted having a fear of going over bridges. Sounds like anxiety to me. Hmmmmm. So I kept working at strengthening my mind and gaining confidence. So much so I decided it was time to face going out in the world. I enrolled in beauty school to get my manicurist license. Absolutely one of the hardest decisions I've ever made.

Many years into seeing my current therapist, he suggested I talk to one of his students about agoraphobia. He was writing his dissertation. I thought it would be an interesting exercise. Besides, he would pay me thirty-five dollars to hear my experiences. So I made an appointment to meet with this guy. He had lots of questions about coping skills, symptoms, and limitations. I think we had gotten through about forty-five minutes and I asked him a question. Had anyone told him about the "upside" of agoraphobia? He said, "Upside?" No one said anything like that. I told him the upside was when I did go out and go to, let's say, Target, I could tell him what aisle everything was in, where the bathrooms were, and how far from the front door I was in any aisle I was in. That made my trips out a little easier, for lack of a better word. I could "reason" with my panic somehow. He thought that was really an interesting take on agoraphobia and panic disorders that he had ever heard before. Well, I'm novel, to say the least.

During the worst part of my agoraphobia I saw an Oprah episode with Lucinda Bassett. Lucinda was the founder of the Midwest Center for Stress and Anxiety. She was someone who had suffered through agoraphobia and anxiety and seemed to have come out on the other side. She had put together a packet and cassette tapes that were available for purchase. I listened to her very carefully. She seemed to know "my" disorder intimately. What was amazing to me was she was going to be traveling all over the country giving seminars. She could get on a plane, travel, talk about her disorder, and help others. I just wanted to be able to drive to local destinations without much fear. She was scheduled to be in Minneapolis. My mom offered to take me. Lucinda was going to be at the Minneapolis Convention Center. It was a pretty big place. Overwhelming for me, but I was determined to go. What struck me as funny and logical was when people came in to find their seats, only the end chairs of each row would fill up. All of us needed to know we could get out quickly. In fact, I think the doors were left open as well. Lucinda was and is a brilliant speaker. She told us of her own struggles and triggers. It gave me some hope that someday, even if all the symptoms of panic and anxiety didn't go away, they would be manageable somehow.

Afterward I had the privilege of meeting her. She was warm and welcoming. My mom bought me the tapes. I listened to them in the order I was supposed to. I used the relaxation tape over and over again so I could get some decent sleep. I practiced the techniques, and I have to say that it helped. I wouldn't say I was completely cured, but I did have a better understanding of how agoraphobia worked. I continued seeing a therapist and practiced, practiced, practiced. The thing I needed to learn most was letting time pass. Or as I say, I want patience and I want it now dammit! Which doesn't work. I also needed to learn how to be kinder to myself. Unfortunately that was the lesson that took the longest. I still work on gentle self-speak. I'm much better with that than ever. If I just could have been kinder to myself growing up, maybe the anxiety disorders wouldn't have had such a strong foundation to attach themselves to. But growing up with my family, such as it was, wasn't conducive to me being kind to myself. If no one was kind to me, how would I learn to be kind to myself, right?

In my lifetime I have worked with several therapists. I've always been a big proponent of trying to understand myself.

When I was sixteen, my parents decided I needed to see a child psychologist. I think my mom wanted me to see this particular doctor because her best friend's daughter was seeing him. Call it a game of psychological keeping up with the Joneses, if you will. I agreed to see him, couldn't hurt, right? The first time I went to his office, I remember thinking this would be helpful. I could talk to someone confidentially and get some understanding of my relationship with my family. He seemed to be a good listener and was compassionate. But there was something about him I didn't trust. After that appointment, I had to pick my mom up at the beauty shop. When I walked in she asked me how it went. Excitedly I told her it was great and some of the things we talked about. She got very quiet. When we left the beauty shop, she started yelling at me how I had embarrassed her in front of everyone in the beauty shop. She was humiliated. It didn't make any sense to me. She had asked me out loud in front of everyone how it went. I evidently made the mistake of thinking she really wanted to know. I guess sending your kid to therapy is not the same as admitting your kid is in therapy.

I saw this doctor for maybe a couple of months. I think every other week. During that time I had found out I was pregnant. As I said before, there was something about him I didn't trust. I told him some things but held back others. I chose not to tell him about the pregnancy. At one of our later sessions, he suggested my parents should join us so we could talk through my frustration with my family. I agreed. It would be great to have someone on my side and explain how I felt. So the following week, my parents joined me. Before any discussion about my frustration started, the doctor said, "I think she's a terribly troubled child and should be institutionalized." What? Where did that come from? I sat there in utter disbelief. I saw everyone's lips moving but couldn't hear anything. My mind was racing! I was reviewing the things I had told him in the past sessions. Absolutely nothing SHOULD have led to me being put in an institution. I remember thinking how lucky I was I didn't say anything about being pregnant. I would've been sent away for sure. I have no recollection what else happened after that. I never went back to his office. My parents didn't commit me but considered it.

Now I have to flash forward to my early twenties. I met someone through a boyfriend. He told me he used to work at a children's mental institution. He said there were a whole bunch of kids that had been committed by this "lying sack of shit child psychologist." The kids would run down the hallway and snatch the toupee off this doctor's head. They called him "Dr. Frankenstein," which was not too far from his real name. This guy also told me that for each kid he had committed, he got some kind of financial kickback from the state. Guess whose doctor that was? Mine! The one my parents chose for me.

I was told this doctor died a slow painful death from multiple sclerosis. I will just leave that alone...

About a year ago I talked to the daughter of my mom's best friend. We talked about that doctor. She said he got her hooked on drugs, and another friend of hers was molested by this guy. I have no proof of those particular things, but there would be no reason she would make this up at this point. I just feel fortunate that I didn't tell that doctor everything. Can you imagine what would have happened to me?

As I said earlier, I met my current therapist in a mental health intake session. He was the one who referred me to a woman therapist. After a couple of sessions, I realized I liked her and trusted her. We were working on the issues of my panic disorder, the agoraphobia before I was housebound, and my relationships with men. It didn't leave a lot of time to talk about the past. We talked a little about my parents and sister, but not much. Remember, I thought growing up the way I did was how everyone grew up. So we focused on my feelings of panic and being out of control. We talked about situational depression, as opposed to chronic depression. The difference being, situational is caused by something specific, chronic is more long term and debilitating. Mine was more of the situational nature.

We mostly talked about the men in my life. Specifically, one man that I was in love with, or thought I was in love with. He was so dangerous. He was an intravenous drug user and a shoplifter or "booster," as he called it. And worst of all an abuser. He would beat me up and belittle me. But let's face it, this was not really so different from my upbringing. When people ask women why they stay in those kinds of relationships, I understand when they say they love the man who is doing this, along with being too afraid to leave because of the consequences they would pay. After a couple of years, I decided to leave. The consequences? Stalking. He stalked me for a long time. I had worked hard to conquer agoraphobia and to go to beauty school. I worked as a manicurist. He would show up at my job. He must've made keys to my car because I would come out and my car would be parked in a completely different area from where I parked it when I got there. I filed restraining orders three separate times. The stalking wouldn't stop. The last court date I had with him, I brought the man I had started dating (later to become my husband/ex-husband), and for some reason he stopped coming around. I was talking to my therapist about these terrible dreams I was having. This stalker person would chase me in my dreams. I would run away screaming and crying. These dreams went on for months. Then one night I was being chased by him in my dream, and I stopped running. I turned around and faced off with him and said, "You don't scare me anymore." That was the last dream about him I had. During that time my therapist encouraged me to bring in a picture of him. I only had one. I brought it in and handed it to her. She asked me how I felt about burning it. I didn't know. She said she thought it would be a healthy step. I agreed. We walked up the third floor of her building, lit the picture with the lighter, and put it in a container like a ceramic bowl or fire-proof trash bin. As good as it felt, in retrospect I wish I hadn't burned the picture. I heard later my therapist got in trouble for it. I do remember hearing someone say, "I smell smoke" when we were burning the picture. Oh well. *Que sera.*

I reconnected with that therapist I was working with in the days of my agoraphobia. It had been around twenty-five years since we had spoken. I had called and left a message. I was hoping she'd remember who I was. If she didn't, that would be OK. When she called me back, she told me she remembered me. She even went as far as to say there were many people she couldn't remember, but I stood out because she thought I was "precious." I was so excited to hear her voice. We spoke for about a half hour. I even got to take the opportunity to tell her how much she meant to me and what an important role she played in my life. If I'm not mistaken, I started to see her regularly when I was twenty-three until around age twenty-seven. Those were some tough years for me. I had horrible anxiety, acting out, or as I prefer to think of it, trying to live my own life and establishing an identity. What I wanted to know was if she had saved notes from our sessions way back then. We did establish that we were both older now. She couldn't believe I was fifty-five. I told her I would be the only one who got older. She laughed. She said a lot of positive things to me. How she felt about our sessions. What she thought was going on in my life back then. There were so many other things going on, I don't even think I revealed the things I'm writing about now. We agreed that back then I would have preferred to hold my breath than cry. When she said all those nice things to me I was so touched. Before we ended our call, she told me I could call or text her if I needed help with getting the notes from our session from the place she worked at then. She also told me I could call or text to let her know how the book was coming along. The boundary of not getting together for coffee was still firmly in place. But I am forever grateful to her for her compassion and help and got to tell her so. That was very important for me. We ended our call; I sat down on my couch and out of the blue started to cry. After thinking about it, the crying was twofold. I was crying because I realized that someone who was important to me understood me, even back then, and didn't judge me. She said she thought I was precious when my parents never could. It's not anything that is going to send me spiraling into depression or even ruin a moment of the rest of my life. But you can see how I would wonder. It's too bad my parents and sister didn't see me for the genuine person I was and am. They are the ones that missed out. But for me there are no "if I only woulda, coulda, SHOULDAS" that go with that.

I have been working with my current therapist on and off for thirty-one years. He has been the "constant" man in my life. He listens to me but doesn't judge me. He "gets" me. In fact, I asked him to write the foreword to my book.

When we first started working together, our focus was on my relationships with men. I was experiencing what I thought was my sexual freedom. What I would learn much later was that I was acting out. Early on he asked me if my father had molested me. The answer was no. I know that at age six I wasn't allowed to sit on his lap anymore. So suddenly I was set aside. We really didn't talk about the physical abuse until recently. There was just so much else to deal with: OCD, PTSD, anxiety, and agoraphobia. Where would we find the time to delve into physical, emotional and mental abuse? Besides, and I have to repeat this, I didn't think of the abuse as anything unusual. Sad, but true. It was "normal" for me. My therapist talked me through many relationships, including my marriage and subsequent divorce. He was proud when I called off my engagement when I was forty-two. He talked me through my anger, my disappointment in my fiancé, and in myself for picking another "winner." At least I recognized it quicker than before.

I think we hit the mother lode the night when I was at my dad and his wife's condo, and it looked like my dad was going to punch his wife. My therapist watched me melt down in his office. Little by little I revealed how I grew up. He said he had an inkling but had no idea how severe things were. We dug deep. There was so much to tell. It was like starting over…almost.

When I told him I was going to write this book, he asked me, was I sure I wanted to do this? My answer was an unequivocal yes. Just last week he told me he admired me for taking on this task. We will continue to work together. There is no one I would rather travel this road with.

Anxiety and fear have held me back for years. My new job is to expand my horizons and go on vacation, drive somewhere unfamiliar. I don't have to like it. I don't have to like how I'm feeling while doing it, I just have to apply all the lessons I've learned to be able to go and do whatever. Look my fear in the eye and say, "So what." All I have to do is trust in my own strength. It's gotten me through a lot.

CHAPTER 3

Dad

I find this to be the most difficult to write. I tried to tackle the subject of my dad several times, but it's so emotionally painful for me. Even just writing that last sentence brings tears to my eyes. How do I get this down on paper? How will I be able to portray the complexity of my feelings for this man I call my father? Most importantly, how can I stop minimizing all the events out of emotional self-preservation? It's all so difficult!

By all accounts, by outside observation, we SHOULD have been a happy family. For as long as I remember, my dad was an angry guy. But he loved "stuff." Golf, tennis, sports, manly-man stuff, material stuff. I'm pretty sure part of his anger had to do with not having sons. I was the closest thing to a jock he would ever have. I played tennis, golf, basketball, and skied. I recall things were difficult between us. When I was seven or eight, my dad bought me a bottle of Tinkerbell perfume. I thought that was nice. I wanted him to love me, and I wanted to love him. He would bring me games when I was sick. In fact, he sat with me all night when I had a 104-degree temperature, putting alcohol and cold water compresses on my head. How could a father that knew how to do that be so angry and violent? It perplexes me forty-plus years later.

My dad would hit me. Not spank me, but hit me in my head and my face, or grab me and fling me around. When I was in junior high he even broke down the bathroom door right off its hinges and dragged me out "caveman style" by my hair. That was because I told him to shut up. He chased me from the living room while my parents' best friends were sitting there. I got to the bathroom, slammed, and locked the door. When I wouldn't come out, BOOM, the door came down, and out I was dragged and thrown into my room. No one did anything. No one intervened. I was kind of used to my mother not doing anything, but their friends?

I was in constant fear of my dad—afraid of his disapproval, his backhanded compliments, his terrible temper, and his fists.

Another junior high incident, not violence really, just something that didn't make sense. I had bought some wire eyeglass frames out of the "For Sale" section of our junior high paper. They cost me a quarter. I had allowance money and I bought them. I was so excited! We all sat down for dinner, and I took them out to show everyone. I put them on and said, "Aren't these cool?" My dad asked to see them. I took them off and handed them to him. He crushed and twisted them. He started yelling what a waste of money they were. How stupid and irresponsible it was to buy. My throat went dry, everything was blurry, and I was screaming in my head (definitely not out loud) those were mine. I bought them. I was shaken and sat there in disbelief, so angry, but too scared to say or do anything about it. It was never spoken about, ever.

I think I spent the first nine years of my life in my room. I was always grounded, mostly for not finishing my dinner. The thing about that, I never got to choose how much food was put on my plate. My dad was a stickler about "the clean plate club." One time I sat down for dinner and nothing smelled good. I know I was feeling "off." I asked if I could have some eggs instead of whatever was being served. My mom went to the stove with a loud, heavy sigh and started making my eggs. My dad started yelling about it not being a "short-order kitchen." How my mother shouldn't have to cook anything special for me. I was ungrateful, etcetera. Well, I got my scrambled eggs but couldn't finish them. Yes, I was grounded and sent to my room. There was a lot of drama that night. About a half hour after being put in my room, I started throwing up. Wouldn't you know it, I had the stomach flu. No wonder I couldn't eat. No apologies from anyone. However, I did hear my mom say, "She's sick."

Well, I've danced around long enough. This will be the hardest thing to write and to see in black and white. I have told the story several times but this will now be in "my permanent record." When I was seventeen, I was living in the basement bedroom of my parents' house. It used to be the storage room. So I fixed it up with a bed, beanbag chair, and TV. My own little refuge. One weekend afternoon I was up in the kitchen eating and watching a documentary on TV. I heard my mom start telling my dad, "You tell her!" My dad came into the kitchen and said, "Your mother wants you to go clean your room." I said I would finish watching the documentary and would be done in ten minutes. He said, "Now!" My mom said, "No, now!" I got upset and told them in ten minutes. Things escalated pretty quickly. My mom and dad were arguing with each other. They were yelling and calling me names. I must have lost my mind because I dropped the f-bomb. I said, "Fuck you." I admit, with my family's violent history, not the best idea.

Next thing I knew my dad had grabbed me by the hood of my sweater and dragged me off the kitchen chair into the living room. I had to hold on to the neck of the sweater because he was choking me. He got on his knees next to me while I lay on the floor. He grabbed me by my hair and started pounding my head into the living room floor. Over and over again I heard my head bounce. I was starting to black out. I knew if I didn't get away, he would kill me for sure. But how? He had such a firm grip. Where was my mom, you ask? She went downstairs. I'm sure she could hear me screaming. She did nothing. I'm not sure how, but I twisted myself around and escaped. I ran out the front door with just the clothes on my back and no shoes. I just kept running. I don't remember where I went, but I used someone's phone and called my boyfriend to come get me. I think he found me walking outside. He got me in the car and drove out to his dorm at the university. His resident advisor came in, took one look at me, and ran for ice. She packed my face, head, and shoulders in ice and was going to call the police. I begged her not to. I told her it would only make things worse. So there I stayed in his dorm, driving myself to high school every day so I could graduate. I think I went home a couple of weeks later to pick up some clothes. My parents wouldn't let anyone come in to help me get my things, so I ran up and down the stairs, bringing things out to the car.

I can tell you that was by far the worst beating I had gotten. I had never felt I was going to die before. But I was afraid, afraid of saying the wrong thing, doing the wrong thing. I had been slapped around quite a bit by my dad. I had gone to school with black eyes and fat lips. Back then no one did anything about it, let alone talked about such things. There weren't many options back then. If I had told anyone, I could have been put into the foster care system but more likely be sent back to my parents' home to suffer the consequences of "telling tales." But honestly, I thought everyone had a family like mine. Why would I think any differently? I didn't live in anyone else's house. I knew my parents didn't generally smack me around when I had friends over. I figured that was just how it was. Sad but true. Maybe even back then I had the ability to compartmentalize. Resiliency? I don't know.

In 1966, my dad almost died from ileitis, now known as Crohn's disease. One night the family was huddled in the northwest corner of the basement because of a terrible storm. My dad suddenly became ill. He and my mom went into the laundry room as my dad was throwing up. I vaguely remember an ambulance being called, but I can't be sure. It may have been something they were talking about. There was a lot of panic. My parents ended up going to the hospital, leaving my sister and me behind. My sister called a friend whose father came and picked us up in the middle of the storm so we wouldn't be alone in our house. We spent the night over there. Either that night or in the following two nights, my dad came near to death. My mom spent her days in the hospital with him. When she finally came home, she said that Dad had turned the corner and was going to be OK. Or as she put it, "He farted." The most beautiful sound she'd ever heard. Pretty funny considering she and my dad spent a lot of time shopping for pine-scented matches and air fresheners. You could hear her say quite often, "Oh my G-d, light a match or something."

My dad coached Little League for years. If you don't have boys, you may as well go coach some. He was known as an all-around great guy as a coach. He loved being a coach. It really didn't help matters that I threw a better curveball than some of his pitchers. He and I were playing catch one day, and I threw a perfect curveball. He was amazed and impressed. He asked me how I knew how to do that. I truthfully didn't know. Too bad Little League didn't let girls play back then. It would have been nice to have more than a moment of my father's approval. Over the years there were Little League reunions. All these men who, as boys, played on my father's teams would come up to him and tell him what he meant to them. How they became the fine men they turned out to be. Oh, it was so warm and fuzzy. He told them he loved being their coach. He loved being able to get to know them and build their character. My question: Who was this guy they loved and admired so much? This was not the dad who I grew up with. My dad was the terrorizer, the intimidator, the bully. How do you think these guys would feel if they knew their beloved coach was beating up his own daughter? It was quite a lot to take in every time one of his former players would gush about him.

I spent a lifetime trying to please him, trying not to cause him to lose his temper, trying to stay out of his way. The problem was, I couldn't seem to do it. There was always something. He was just so angry or judgmental or dismissive. Even when I was a grown woman living on my own, there would be problems. I tried to be the best daughter I knew how to be when I was around him. Sure, there were some days I did what I wanted to do, I was on my own after all. In my early twenties, I invited my family over for dinner. I had made barbecued chicken and whatever went with that. My dad took a piece of chicken, tasted it, and looked right at my mom and said, "This is good. Why can't you cook like this?" My heart just sank. Let the fighting begin. That was pretty indicative of the belittling that went on. Oh, what a terrible night that was. But the chicken really was good.

When I was three or four my dad wanted to cut my toenails and fingernails. I always sat still except for this one time. A piece of skin had overgrown by my baby toe on my right foot. I would play with the skin, especially when I was stressed. How does a three- or four-year-old get stressed? When her parents are fighting and when she knows she could get drawn into the middle of it without even trying. This little piece of skin soothed me. I know it sounds crazy, but it did. So when it came time to cut my toenails, my dad saw the piece of skin. He told me he was going to cut it off. I begged him not to and took off running. He chased me through the house. I finally dove under my parents' king-sized bed. I was crying and begging. He somehow reached me, grabbing me by my ankle, and dragging me out from under the bed. He sat on me, yes sat on me, grabbed my foot, and cut off the piece of dead skin. I remember feeling violated somehow. But of course at three or four, I didn't have the words for it. I just knew it didn't feel right to me that he could do that.

After my mom died, Dad would come to my condo for dinner. He was the only parent I had left, and I wanted to try to have a decent relationship with him. Every time he came over, he was rude. I realize now that I was "SHOULDING." I thought I SHOULD have him over, I thought I SHOULD try to have a normal relationship with him. I now realize it takes two to forge a relationship. He would talk about the most inappropriate things. Picking up women, should he buy condoms, etcetera. Sex was always a topic he liked to talk about. It was so lascivious. But he was always like that. He didn't seem to have any common sense as to what was appropriate to talk to his daughter about. So eventually, the dinners stopped. I couldn't listen to the sex stuff or to his opinion of me. Even though I had a career of my own, a company of my own, he thought I should be selling cars. We all know how people feel about car salesmen. They're considered lower than ambulance-chasing attorneys. Why would this be something he would want me to do? I didn't find it flattering at all. But then he had a lot of opinions about me that were unflattering.

My dad remarried a year and a half after my mom died. That is a whole chapter on its own. His remarriage gave us an extended step-family. One of the stepgrandkids had a Bar Mitzvah. I was invited and brought my serious boyfriend with me. I had on a beautiful, long, loose-fitting purple dress with a duster-type drapey jacket. We were walking from place to place. There was a lot to see and do at the party. My boyfriend and I sat down at the table with my dad. Everyone was having a great time. Out of the blue my dad said to me, "You know you're getting fat, don't you?" What? I couldn't believe what I was hearing. I turned to him and said, "You are not Estelle Getty. You have not had a stroke and this is not *The Golden Girls*." He looked at me like I was crazy. My boyfriend and I left very shortly thereafter. I never brought it up with my dad because…why? It wouldn't change him into a better person. Why bother?

Our first Passover with the stepfamily was quite an experience. Each family has their own traditions and the way they go about doing things. This stepfamily liked to put on shows and dress in costumes. Not something my family was used to, but it was interesting. So there we were sitting, new to the group. My stepbrother was leading the service. I was sitting next to my dad. I noticed he was becoming agitated. I leaned over and asked him if he was OK. He said, "This is not right. They're not doing it right." (Referring to the service.) This coming from a man who claims he was "just a Christian scientist" because his mother raised him that way (including pork roast on Rosh Hashanah). But he was really insistent we be raised in Judaism. He became louder and more insistent that this was all wrong. I leaned over and quietly told him to lower his voice and that every family has their own way of celebrating Passover and this was their way. Well, next he turned on me. In front of G-d and everybody, he started yelling at me how stupid I was and that I wasn't going to tell him what to do. He was belittling and humiliating me. I was stunned he would be that openly rude to me in front of the "new family." I got up from the table, got my purse, and left. I came home and had my own Passover Seder. Of course the next day there was no apology.

Family gatherings were never very pleasant. I just held out hope year after year things would change. What is the definition of insanity? Doing the same thing over and over again, expecting a different outcome. That was my impression of my family gatherings, whether with immediate family or stepfamily. It seemed that the worst things happened in the Rosh Hashanah/Yom Kippur timeframe.

As I got into my forties, my excuse for continuing to go to these painful, dysfunctional holiday or family gatherings was that my dad was in his eighties and how much time would be left? Or in other words, how much time could possibly be left? So I "SHOULD" myself into going. I would help serve food and help clear the dishes. I figured that it was harder to hit a moving target when it came to all the negativity. It didn't always work. I would go to these things and try to stay under the radar.

Ah, my fortieth birthday! I had waited my entire life to turn forty. Somehow I had the impression that once I turned forty everything would be a breeze. For me, forty represented an inauguration of wisdom, health, peace, and security. Ha! I was about to learn there really is no "magic" age.

I wanted to throw a fun, unique fortieth birthday party for myself—something that my friends would love as much as I would. There was only one answer. Casey Jones. For the non-Minnesotans who are reading this, Casey Jones was a local TV personality. He dressed like a train conductor and would "arrive on track 11." When I was growing up, he had a noontime show called "Lunch with Casey." He and his sidekick, Roundhouse Rodney, would perform skits and songs, have lunch, introduce cartoons, and just generally have fun. For me, his show was the only time there was no fighting, screaming, or hitting. I loved him for that.

About a month before my birthday, I was at my dad's, and he and his wife asked me what I wanted for my fortieth birthday. What kind of party? So I told them. I want to have Casey Jones at my party. It didn't take more than a minute. My dad started yelling at me. "That's the dumbest thing I've ever heard." Let the berating begin. I told him I wasn't asking him to pay for it, but that was what I was going to do. I don't know why I was so stunned by his venomous reaction. I could feel myself start to shake and feel sick. I had to leave…fast! I think he was still going on and on when I put on my coat, picked up my purse, and left. I can honestly tell you I don't remember the drive home. The next thing I remember is sitting on top of the kitchen counter in my house, talking to a friend on the phone, crying hysterically. After calming down, I realized that I could do this on my own. I didn't need any help.

Fate is an interesting thing. That same week of the fight, my dad and his wife used their anniversary gift certificate for their Amtrak train trip to Stillwater. While on the train, they struck up a conversation with a younger couple. They started talking about their kids and the ages of all their kids. Somewhere in the conversation, my stepmother mentioned that I was turning forty and wanted Casey Jones at my party. I suppose you could say it was a natural progression... maybe. Casey Jones, trains...you know. Well, it turned out that this couple was working on a local campaign and had just contacted the guy who played Casey Jones (Roger Awsumb) to help them on the campaign. They just happened to have Casey's number. The next day my stepmother called, told me the story, and gave me his number. I was so excited! I called him and he agreed to be at my fortieth birthday party. I invited twenty-five people. Some came dressed as little kids, and we were nine years old and in a bubble for three hours on a Saturday afternoon. There is a video of me looking out the window, seeing him arrive and screaming, "He's here!" I was running down the stairs to greet him. It was such a thrill! There he was, dressed in his conductor overalls with his trusty ukulele, which meant he was going to sing too! My heart was pounding. If that wasn't enough, he did something that I didn't expect, something that he didn't even know would mean the world to me. In all the hubbub of his entrance, my sister walked up to him and said, "I'm her much older sister. So you can imagine how much longer I've been watching you than she has." For me, I could hear a pin drop, everything went quiet until he looked at me, put his arm around me, and said, "Let's go meet your friends." He didn't even address my sister. Well, if I didn't love him before, I certainly loved him now. And off we went.

I took great pains to make my fortieth birthday like a kids' party. Macaroni and cheese, shoestring potatoes, milk cartons with bendy straws, and cake and ice cream. I even had a working train running around the food table. What a fun day! It is still, to date, the best party I've ever thrown. My friends still talk about it. I didn't get to have a private moment with Casey to let him know what he meant to me. That he was a peaceful part of my life. He hugged me and then he had to leave.

Something else came from that party. I was going to pay Casey his guest appearance fee, but my dad had already done it. Hmmmm, odd. I asked him about it the next day. He told me he realized that the people he saw at my party were people he had seen with me most of my life. This is a man that told me from when I was eight or nine that I couldn't get along with anybody. I always thought that was a strange thing to say since my friends have been with me for years. So I guess that was some kind of admission that he had been wrong about something. He also thought it was a great party. He was surprised during the sing-along portion. We all knew the words to all of Casey's songs. It was a great day all around. Did that mean my dad was coming around? Nah. But it was nice for that day.

At eighty-one, Dad had quadruple bypass surgery. Pretty stressful for all of us. But he came through with flying colors. One of his proudest moments was when the doctor told him that he had a hard time getting the vein out of my dad's leg because his legs were so muscular. My dad, the jock. Fewer things were more important to him than his physical appearance and ability to work out. It would be months after his bypass that he would be able to work out again. But he did it. As he got later into his eighties, there were some health scares: pneumonia, spinal stenosis. As he got into his nineties, there was what appeared to be bladder cancer. He was scheduled for surgery to have what they thought was a tumor removed. We all gathered at the hospital and waited for him to be prepped for surgery. They said it would probably be an hour. So my sister, stepmother, and I went to the cafeteria to get something to eat. As we sat down to patiently wait, the pager we were carrying started blinking with a "come back to the waiting room" message. It had only been twenty minutes, maybe a half hour. We all looked at each other. Nothing much was said. We gathered our stuff and went back to the waiting room and did just that, waited. About a half hour later the doctor came out and said it was a blood clot. As soon as he touched it, it dissipated. I know we were all expecting the doctor to tell us Dad was dead. But no, the Energizer Bunny lived on! As we went back to his hospital room, I suddenly lost it. I started crying. I don't know if it was relief or fear. I guess it doesn't matter. My sister was nice enough to put her arms around me. I stopped crying, and we went to his room.

Dad had to go in for all kinds of follow-up appointments. My sister took him to some; I took him to some. This one particular time I picked him up at his condo, helped him into my car, as I always did. I loaded his walker in the back of my car and off we went to his doctor. We went up to the second floor in the elevator. He had this checkup, and after he got dressed, I went into the room to be a second pair of ears and take notes as to what the doctor thought and instructions for Dad. We left the office, and Dad was using his walker, and I was walking slowly with him. We were heading toward the elevator, and he looked to his right and saw the steps. He smiled and said to me, "Why don't we go down the steps, it would be quicker." I said, smiling back, "The only way you're getting down those steps is if I throw you down and throw your walker after you." We got in the elevator and he replied, "I guess that would make us even." I heard myself take a sharp inhale and gasp. I went blank for a couple of seconds. Then I realized he remembered what he had done to me. I could barely breathe, barely speak. I know I paid attention to my driving, but I don't remember anything but a low humming noise in my ears.

Dad ended up in the hospital several times the year before he died and up until the end. One day he looked at me from his hospital bed, and he was crying. He said he didn't think anybody would care about him. I think he was coming to terms, or at least what he thought was coming to terms, with what kind of father he was.

His last hospital stay was really awful. He had pneumonia and dysphagia. Everything he swallowed went right into his lungs. There was no coming back from this one. After a week or so, he was transferred to a nursing home, and then into hospice care. I went to see him every day. He was disoriented. Every time he saw a commercial on TV about food he would try to get out of bed, saying he needed to go grocery shopping. I reminded him that his wife was ordering groceries online and that they would deliver it to them. He would calm down and go back to sleep. I told the nurses and caregivers to say that to him.

The day before he died, I went to visit him and knew it wouldn't be much longer. I took him by his hands and asked him to look at me. He opened his eyes and looked right into mine. I said, "I forgive you for being an awful father." He squeezed my hands and closed his eyes. I stayed a little while longer and then I went home.

The following morning around eight thirty I went over to see him. He was really weak. His eyes were closed. I don't even think he knew I was there. I sat on the bed and didn't say much. I kissed him on his forehead and left. At one o'clock I got a call from my sister saying Dad had died. I told her I would be right there. I called my best friend and asked her to meet me there. I needed her by my side. Little did I know how much. You would think this would be the end of the story, but it's not. The saga continues in the stepfamily chapter.

CHAPTER 4

Mom

How did I not see what was going on in my own house? How did it not become crystal clear to me until I was fifty-one? Growing up in my house was not easy. But what did I know? I thought everybody's family was like mine. I always had nice things. In retrospect, I realized that the things were more important to everyone but me. Second to that was the appearance of our "perfect, happy family."

I started taking swimming lessons pretty early on. I think I was six. There was a male instructor in his thirties. There was something about him I didn't like or trust. When my mom would leave me in the pool area for the lesson, she would go into another room where she would wait. I couldn't see her, and she couldn't see me. The minute she was out of my sight, I started to cry. I was scared. Of what? I wasn't sure. Very early on if I cried, this instructor would take me to the shallow end of the pool and spank me. He would tell me to stop crying, or he would continue to spank me. I was, of course, inconsolable, and he would continue to spank me. When I could finally calm myself down, he would take me into the pool. Mind you, these were not private lessons. There were other kids there. This instructor would spit in the pool and push his spit down to the deep end. It was gross. It was vile. The second time I cried, I know my mom saw him grab me, take me to the shallow end, and start spanking me. She saw, I know she did! I screamed for her, and she turned around and walked out. I realized in that instant I was on my own. On more than one occasion, he would have me floating on my back in the middle of the pool. If I became anxious or what he deemed difficult, he would push my head up and out of the water so that I would go under. I would flail around to try to save myself, and he would make sure I would go under again. Of course then I would start to cry and you know what happened next...I don't remember much else about it. I don't know if I quit swimming or the amount of lessons were over. I can tell you to this day I am not fond of swimming. I can swim, but I am much better standing in a pool or treading water without getting my head wet.

Next I tried skating. I was around seven. I liked the teacher. I liked that she was patient and kind. I recall wearing winter coats with furry cuffs and collars with warm gloves. It was very "Currier and Ives." I skated for years. I liked it. I had good balance. I wasn't really interested in becoming a professional skater. I just wanted to be able to skate well and not get hurt. Well, we all know that's good in theory. I was skating one afternoon, fell, and somebody skated over my finger opening up a gash to the bone. All that blood...ugh! I had to be taken to the doctor and have stitches. Skating was not the same after that. I became scared. Remember, I was afraid of everything all of the time.

For as long as I could remember, my mom worked. She had a home office where she wrote a cake-decorating magazine. There was a main office where she delivered her work. I would go with her quite often. The ladies there were so nice. They were all so friendly to me. One lady always had candy in a bowl on her desk. Every time I was there, she would smile at me and offer me some. I would wander around and say hi to everyone. I could even go into the warehouse and jump into a pile of packing worms, just like leaves on a fall day. I was happy when I was there.

Mom had gone out to dinner at a downtown restaurant. Several days later she didn't feel well. She thought she had food poisoning. She went to the doctor and was diagnosed with non-Hodgkin's lymphoma sometime in the 1980s. I'm not sure exactly when. The family sat down with her doctor, and I'm sure we all heard different things. I know what I heard was at the age she was at the time it wouldn't be a "life-shortening illness." After an X-ray, the doctor found a tumor wrapped around her stomach and at the base of her heart. Surgery was scheduled, followed by chemotherapy. I don't remember her being sick from the chemo, but she did lose her hair. She had gotten a couple of different wigs to cover her bald head. Oddly enough, a couple funny things come to mind. The first being my sister and I playing catch/keep away with the wigs and telling Mom she was "flipping her wig." The second was when she wasn't wearing the wig, she wasn't entirely bald. She had one curl right above her forehead that wouldn't fall out. All I could think of was this poem Mom used to recite when I was growing up: "There was a little girl with a curl right in the middle of the forehead. When she was good, she was very, very good; and when she was bad, she was horrid." How's that for irony? So my mom would take scarves and wrap them "Aunt Jemima style," like the picture on the Aunt Jemima products, and pull that curl forward so it would hang out of the scarf. Odd what I remember and don't remember from that time.

The following story I wasn't sure I should include in my book. But I realized what was said to me by my mother was nothing I would have ever wished to hear. But it ended up being a secret I thought I had to keep. Revealing what was said would serve no one and hurt one person, my sister. After all the terrible things my sister has said and done, I still felt some kind of duty to protect her. A "SHOULDING," if you will. But this book is to let people know harboring secrets serves no one. Staying silent about abuse, whether it be physical, mental, or emotional just hurts the "secret keeper." So it is in that vein I finally let the last secret of my mother's cruelty go…

Several years after my mother's cancer diagnosis, she called and asked me to come over to her house. When I got there, she was sitting at the kitchen table with a piece of paper, a pen, and her jewelry pouch. She asked me to sit down at the table with her. She said she wanted to know what I wanted from the house and from her jewelry bag so she could earmark it for me. I told her that more than anything I didn't want to have this conversation. She said I needed to tell her, "Because in your grief, your sister will roll all over you." I was shocked at how cold that statement was regarding her own daughter. She said it so matter-of-factly. It's not that I necessarily disagreed, but it was so shocking. And I realized at that moment I thought I had a secret to keep. My sister didn't need to know what my mom said or how she felt about her. I felt sick. The only people I told were my closest friends. I told them how awful it was and how my sister SHOULD never be told. It has pained me for over twenty-two years. Now that moment in time doesn't have to be my responsibility any-more. In fact, it never was. It was just another "SHOULDING" of my own doing.

I know we all breathed a sigh of relief when Mom was can-cer-free for a couple of years. In fact, we had a party to celebrate. I had invited a bunch of people to my mom and dad's to celebrate my mom's birthday. I had spent months crocheting her an afghan that matched the bright-colored furniture in their basement. Every waking moment, every break at work, I crocheted. I finished it the day before the party. I wrapped it in a big box with a bow. The day of the party I brought the box over and put it downstairs where the guests would be putting their gifts. It was a lovely party. Mom and Dad were happy to have their friends around. We ate, talked, drank and then came time to open the gifts. My mom opened each gift with care. She would read the card and thank each person profusely. Then it came time to open my gift. I was so excited to see the look on her face! She opened it, picked up the corner of the afghan, read my card and looked at me, and said thank you, sort of in a mono-tone. Anticlimactic would be an understatement. I thought she'd be so excited. I guess I was wrong. Maybe she didn't like it at all. I couldn't tell. After more socializing, people started to leave. After the last guest was gone my mom came up to me to tell me she loved my gift and didn't think she should show any more excitement than the other gifts because she didn't want to make her guests feel bad. What? I didn't get it, but that's the way she thought she should play it. She did use that afghan all the time. At least that's something.

When I was in second grade, I could make a choice of hot lunch (green tickets) or cold lunch (red tickets). My mom and I used to review the school's lunch menu every week in the newspaper. I would get to choose my favorite for hot lunch, like creamed turkey on mashed potatoes, grilled cheese, and hot dogs. The other days my mom would pack me a lunch in a brown bag with my name on it. One day my mom told me she was too busy to pack my lunch for the end of the week and could I go ask the lunch ladies in the kitchen to make some plain spaghetti noodles without the meat sauce so she wouldn't have to pack me a lunch that day. So at school the following day, I asked if I could go to the bathroom. I did just that. When I came out of the bathroom I realized the lunchroom was right next door, and the lunch ladies were there. So I went and asked them if it was possible to make some plain noodles for me on that Friday. I told them my mom was too busy to pack me a lunch. I'm sure they thought I was crazy but said they could do that. I said thank you and went back to class. I told my teacher I had stopped in the kitchen and talked to the lunch ladies on the way back from the bathroom. She said, "You did what?" I explained it again and told her my mom had asked me to do it. My teacher was really angry. I didn't understand why. I was just doing what my mom had asked me to do. What she told me I SHOULD do. So the spaghetti with meat sauce day came around, and my teacher walked with me through the lunch line. When the lunch ladies saw me they said, "Oh, oh. There she is. Get the spaghetti noodles." My teacher said, "No, she's going to eat what everybody else is eating." So they dished out the spaghetti and meat sauce, and my teacher followed me to a table where she made me sit by myself. She told me if I didn't eat all of what was in front of me, there would be no recess. So no recess there was. I tried but gagged on the spaghetti and meat sauce. My teacher called my mother. My mother denied ever telling me to ask for plain noodles. So not only was there no recess, my mom told my dad, and I was grounded for a week. Now really, why would a second grader make up such a story? And I was punished both at school and at home. Really unfair. And why did she lie? I wouldn't understand or even see this pattern until I was fifty-one.

When I was little, my mom liked to brush my hair. She especially liked to put my hair in really tight pigtails. She would pull them so tight! If I would complain she was hurting me, she would hit me in the head with the brush, or she would clap me on my ears really hard. I remember coming back from sleep away summer camp and telling her how good it felt to do my own hair and feel independent. I didn't realize then it was more about not getting hit in the head anymore.

In elementary school I started taking dance lessons: jazz, tap, ballet, and acrobatics. I loved it! I loved learning. I loved the movement. It made me happy. In junior high I started dancing with the Minnesota Dance Theater and School. Two friends and I would take the bus to Dinkytown, walk from the bus stop down the block to the dry cleaners. We would walk up the stairs behind the dry cleaners, and there was the studio. It was a very exciting place to be. It was completely different from other places I had taken lessons. It was more prestigious because some of the students had a chance to audition for the Minnesota Dance Theater's production of Loyce Houlton's *The Nutcracker Suite*. I danced at the school for a couple of years and then decided to audition for *The Nutcracker*. There were so many young girls and boys there to try out to be a soldier or a mouse. They knew they were only going to pick seven of us out of the hundred that were there. I was nervous and so excited! Who knew? It could have been the beginning of a career. So there were several rounds of auditions. Then we all sat there waiting to hear if we had been chosen. My mom had driven me there and was sitting up in the balcony with the other parents. They started calling out names. I was one of them! I was going to be a mouse. How exciting! I would work hard and learn so much. I would work in the dance theater company and earn my way to other auditions and parts. It seemed the sky was the limit. They asked the parents of those of us who were chosen to join them downstairs. We all sat together and were told what was expected. There would be four rehearsals a week. The parents would give out programs. There were other things, but I really don't remember what they were. Oh, how exciting. The theater! What a beginning.

My mom and I walked to our blue Buick LeSabre. I got in and was excitedly talking about being in the production. My mother turned to me and said, "Just be satisfied in knowing you made it." I asked her what she meant by that. She told me she wasn't going to drive me to the studio four times a week. I told her I'd take the bus like I had before. And she told me she wasn't going to let me do that and repeated the "just be satisfied in knowing you made it" statement. And that was the end of the Minnesota Dance Theater and School.

When I was dancing at the Minnesota Dance Theater, I would stop at Vescio's Restaurant and have a side order of pizza and something to drink. Every time I was there, Frank Vescio would come over and talk to me. We got to be really good friends. He would see me getting ready to go outside and wait for the bus. In the winter he would give me a cup of hot chocolate to make sure I stayed warm. I asked my parents to go to Vescio's one night to meet my friend Frank. They thanked him for taking good care of me. Many years later Frank died. My parents and I went to Vescio's Restaurant, different location, same family owners. I noticed Frank's son was working, and I wanted to tell him how sorry I was about his dad and how much his dad meant to me. He came to the table, and I started to say how sorry I was. My mother interrupted and said how she had asked Frank to watch over me while I was at the Dinkytown location and what good friends she was with Frank. My ears were ringing. I was so angry. She was lying! I didn't know why she would be like that. I had introduced her to Frank. Frank and I were friends. I didn't know what to do. I just sat there while she lied. I felt sick to my stomach. She had just trampled on my special relationship with Frank. I was afraid to speak up. I know I probably SHOULD have. This would not be the first or last time she would take credit for things that didn't belong to her. I would find out much later what lengths she would go to be in a "sick" competition with me. The problem with competition, don't you need at least two players? I know that I wasn't participating. But her competition would rear its ugly head many times over.

After the Minnesota Dance Theater, I didn't know if I wanted to dance anymore. It was such a blow not to be dancing in *The Nutcracker Suite*. Even now when I see advertising for Lisa Houlton's production of *The Nutcracker*, I can barely breathe. I will never know if I would have gone on to choose dance as a career or get tired of it on my own. (For my fifty-fifth birthday present my best friend bought tickets for the Minnesota Dance Theater's fifty-year anniversary production of *The Nutcracker Suite*. I was prepared for whatever feelings would come my way. I can honestly say, it was magical and very healing for me).

I think it was my mother that found the Andahazy School of Ballet. It was close to our house and much more "convenient." My parents told me if I really loved dancing, I could take classes there. So I thought I'd try it. I was balancing school, skiing, basketball, and Vocaleers (choir and volleyball) at the same time. But I did want to dance. Andahazy Ballet was worlds away from the Minnesota Dance Theater. Andahazy was a strict Russian ballet school and dance Company, while the Minnesota Dance Theater and School was much more lighthearted and thrived on the creativity of their staff and students. Mr. Andahazy was tough. He didn't smile much. He was aggressive, yelled, and belittled the students. Suffice it to say if I wanted to be treated like that, I could just stay home. But I wanted to give it a try. I think I lasted one month. I was at the barre doing a plié and my knee locked. The same knee I had injured the previous year skiing. Mr. Andahazy came up to me and instructed me to straighten my legs and stand up straight. I told him I couldn't, my knee was locked. I told him I had injured it skiing. He told me I had to choose between dancing or skiing. I couldn't do both. He walked around with a stick that he would hit the ground to keep time to the music. When I told him I liked both skiing and dancing, he hauled off and hit my leg with that pointy stick. That was my last day at Andahazy. I had danced for nine years, and no instructor had ever hurt me until that day. I gave up dance. I didn't know what else to do or where else to go where I would feel safe. So again, I will never know if I could've had a career in dance. Disco doesn't count.

I started taking guitar lessons around the same time I was dancing. I took private lessons from a woman who taught out of her home. She taught me a lot. At some point she stopped giving lessons, so I found myself a new teacher at a local music store. I think my instructor played in a band. He was very talented, patient, and easygoing. I was about thirteen or fourteen. He was a much older, twenty-five or twenty-six. I loved to listen to him play. My only problem, I had a really hard time reading music. No matter how hard I tried, I just couldn't learn that way. So he started teaching me by having me imitate what he was doing. He told me what the chords were called, how to position my hands, and how to use a capo. He wrote the names of the chords in my music book. I would practice at home and come back the following week to show him how far I had come. He would tell me he was impressed, proud even. After a few lessons we would play songs together. I just loved the time there. We were wrapping up one lesson, and I asked him to play "April." He had played it for me before, but I just loved the way he played and sang it. I wanted to learn it so we could play together before all my lessons were done. He finished singing, I applauded and said thank you. I walked out of the lesson room, and there was my mother waiting for me, staring at me. She had a strange look on her face. Something was wrong. We went out to the car and she started yelling at me. "You were flirting! I didn't send you here to flirt. I sent you here to learn to play guitar." I assured her I was not flirting. I was learning to play guitar. She countered with, "Wait until I tell your father." There was a lot of that "wait until your father gets home, I'm telling your father what you did" kind of thing growing up. It never did bode well for me. I usually ended up being slapped around and grounded. How could this happen? I didn't do anything. I was learning. I was happy. I was comfortable. I felt safe with my instructor. How could this end up costing me? That was my last lesson.

I continued to ski. I loved flying down the hills in my orange ensemble. I was pretty good at it. I was skiing with the local ski school for a while. Early morning buses, all day skiing all over the state and into Wisconsin. When ski school ended, then I would only ski periodically.

I sang in my junior high choir. We not only had a choir, but the choir also competed in volleyball. I loved singing. I had a high tenor to second soprano range. That allowed me to sing all kinds of harmonies. We did Christmas concerts around the Twin Cities and one big school concert every year. Our choir teacher made it fun. We sang in different languages in two of the three concerts I was in. It was a lot of work and a lot of fun. I tried out for the school talent show. A friend of mine (one of "my family of choice") played piano while we sang. We didn't make it into the show, but that was all right. I was very nervous. Believe it or not, with all of my dance, guitar, and singing experience, I had terrible stage fright.

Our school concert was coming up and the theme was "Around the World in Just One Night," which was not to be mistaken for "Around the World a Second Time" the following year. The choir director approached me and asked me if I wanted to play a stewardess to give the flight instructions before we took off on our around the world tour. I said absolutely. I called Northwest Airlines and spoke to someone about the exact "seat and tray tables in their upright and locked position" speech. The woman I spoke to gave me her name, and I asked her if she wanted to come see the show. She said she did. I left her a ticket; she didn't show up. But that's OK. I went and bought the stewardess-like outfit complete with beret and white go-go boots. When the show started I entered from the back of the auditorium and walked all the way up the center aisle to the stage. I grabbed a microphone and welcomed everyone aboard. I gave the whole spiel about emergencies, etcetera, and then the show would start. I think the concert was about one and a half hours. We did the show twice in two days. It was amazing. I learned a lot of different languages and learned about other cultures. It was fun. I was happy.

Since this chapter is about my mom, I have to flash forward from my junior high years of 1972 to 1974, to my twenties, somewhere around1982 to 1983. I don't know how this particular conversation got started. When I was living on my own in my first apartment, I was on the phone with my mom. I don't even remember what we were talking about, but she brought up the junior high concert. Odd, but OK...Out of the blue she says, "When you didn't make the talent show, I called the school to let them know you should have made it." My reaction was, you did what? Her response was, "You didn't think you got that stewardess part on your own, did you?" Even now at fifty-five, just writing it makes me sick to my stomach and makes my head hurt. My first reaction was I would have to track down the choir teacher and everyone on the school board and apologize. I wanted to tell them all I didn't know she had done this. My mind was racing! My second reaction was, why did I have to know this? What difference did it make now? What was the point of her telling me? My next reaction, did she really call the school or was she trying to take credit for yet another thing I had done? I did try to track down the choir teacher, and I found out he had died a couple years before. Now I would never know the true story.

For my sixteenth birthday, my parents asked me to pick out a restaurant I wanted to go to. They wanted to know if I wanted my boyfriend to come with us. Of course I did. I picked a nice restaurant, someplace I could get all dressed up. I picked Steak and Ale. It was beautiful inside. It felt very grown up to me. We got to our table, and the hostess handed us our menus. So much to choose from! I picked out what was special to fit the occasion. I think it was a steak-and-seafood combination. Everyone got along, no fighting, no belittling. All in all it was a lovely evening. I thanked them for dinner. The next day I was sitting with my mom. I was talking about what a nice birthday dinner I had had. I told her how beautiful I thought the restaurant was and how nice it was they took me there. Honestly, in my mind it gave me hope that we could be a happy family. She turned to me with a strange but stern look on her face. She said, "Well, you SHOULD be happy because you ordered the most expensive thing on the menu. That took a lot of nerve." Well, so much for my hopes that I might have a happy family. I can remember the sick feeling in my stomach and feeling like someone let the air out of the balloon. I remember everything went absolutely silent in that moment, like there wasn't enough air in the room to sustain breath. I also remember thinking that it was my birthday. You didn't tell me what I SHOULDN'T order. From that day forward until both of my parents died, every time I went to a restaurant with them

I looked at prices first. It was probably a good thing I became allergic to seafood when I was twenty-three and stopped eating red meat when I was thirty.

There was a lot of shaming of me from my mother. She used guilt and manipulation. I just thought that was par for the course in being Jewish. Her using guilt was not at all lighthearted. It was to try and bend me to her will. I was working full-time at The Limited. On my day off, my boss called and said she needed me to do something for her. I asked my mom if I could borrow her car (because I didn't have a car of my own). She said OK. I drove out to the store, ran the errand my boss needed me to run, stopped at a shoe store, and then drove home. When I got there, my mom was in the front yard in a two-tone blue Hawaiian print bikini standing next to the waterfall sprinkler. She was splashing herself with water. I stopped the car in the driveway, got out, and she said, "I was invited to our country club, but I couldn't go because you had the car. So this is my pool, *this* is my pool." I was only gone a couple of hours if that. I told her she had plenty of time to get to the club. Honestly, it was two o'clock in the afternoon. There were no cell phones back then, but she could have called the store to let me know she needed me to come home right away. So there she stood, in her bikini next to the sprinkler repeating, "This is my pool."

In my mid-twenties my mom asked me to come over to her house. She wanted to know how I did my makeup. She said she wanted her eyes to look "dirty" like mine. I figured she actually meant smoky. I took her into the bathroom and applied my eye shadow. I have to tell you, this is not even 20-20 hindsight. It gave me a really creepy and uneasy feeling. I was applying the color. She had heavier skin on her eyelids (like I do now at age fifty-five). The shadow was hard to apply as was the notion that she wanted her look to be like mine. My mom was always a fashion-plate. But I couldn't shake this feeling. Then it occurred to me, she was in competition for my youth. She had borrowed clothes from me to wear to parties, even though she had closets full of clothes. Just the thought of her being in competition for my youth made me queasy. And overthinking it, as I have been known to do, did that mean I was in competition with her? Had I somehow done something to spur that on? My con-clusion? Absolutely not. It takes two to be in a true competition. So what would this be called? I didn't want to know. All I was sure of is that I didn't want any part of it. I put myself on notice to watch for this kind of behavior in the future. I did not want to participate in any way.

In 1985, I had started dating someone I knew from high school. He would later become my husband, then my ex-husband. We bought a house and moved in together in 1986. It was a cute little cookie-cutter house. It was a three-bedroom, one-bathroom rambler. I absolutely loved making that house our own. We decided to have a Passover at our new house. My mom was not thrilled with that idea because we were not a married couple yet. But even with her objections, we went ahead and invited people. There ended up being twenty-one people that year. That's a lot of people with only one bathroom. All I wanted to do was host a beautiful Seder and enjoy Passover. For me Passover is my favorite holiday, just edging out Thanksgiving. I set a beautiful table and was really looking for-ward to greeting my guests and having a wonderful time. Everyone was so happy to be there, except my mother. When she arrived, it was apparent there was something off about her. She was kind of snarky and short tempered. She was talking negatively and being just plain rude to my guests. We got through the Seder with some interrup-tions from my mother. As I cleared the table to get ready for coffee and dessert, I pulled her aside to talk to her about how rude she was being. I spoke quietly as not to let others hear. I asked her what was wrong, what was making her act like she was. She became irate and locked herself in the only bathroom we had. With twenty other peo-ple in the house, this was not good at all! I did go knock on the door of the bathroom to see if she was OK. I think I got a curt "fine," and there she stayed. So we went on with dessert and coffee. I figured it was twenty minutes later she made her way out of the bathroom. She told my dad they were leaving, then they were gone. Of course, there was no excuse in the world to make up for the discomfort of my guests. I was still discovering how much attention my mother, my family for that matter, needed. Just another pattern I didn't become aware of until much later.

My boyfriend proposed in 1987. What a joyous thing to plan a wedding, right? Maybe other people…mine, not so much. First we told our families. Then we were off and running planning the wedding. Besides the date, my fiancé left pretty much everything up to me. Flowers, music, bridesmaids, food, etcetera. I ended up doing a lot of this with my mother. I wanted a smaller wedding because my fiancé had been married and divorced. I thought that would be the tasteful thing to do. What I SHOULD do? I had a good idea what I wanted invitations to look like, something simple with an abstract flower on it. So off my mother and I went to look at invitations. There they were, after looking through several sample books, the perfect invitation. Off-white with a light coral colored abstract flower on the front. Beautiful and reasonably priced. I loved them. I took the sample out, I knew this was it! I told my mom we could stop looking, that I found exactly what I was looking for. She took one look at it and said, "No, that's not what you're going to use for an invitation." She didn't have any valid reason, just no. So she proceeded to pick out and order what she wanted. I just didn't want to fight. It was a run of the mill off-white invitation with gold embossed lettering. I figured the message would be the same, "come to our wedding." Besides, I didn't have the energy for what I thought would turn into a big battle.

Flowers were a little easier. She seemed to like my choices. I just wanted them to be low-key and tasteful. The dresses, well that was interesting. I gave my mom, sister, and my maid of honor a color pallet. Any shade of rose. I asked them all to be tasteful and more importantly be something they could wear again. I didn't want bridesmaid looking dresses. Just cocktail length, anything in the rose family. Sounds easy, right? Everyone gets to buy what fits their taste. I couldn't have made it easier. The only one to handle the task with no drama was my maid of honor. She had someone make her a dress in a rose color. Easy-peasy. My sister and mother, on the other hand, were talking about embellishments and poofs. So I ended up having to go shopping with both of them. My sister bought a beautiful medium rose-colored dress with a wraparound belt. My mother bought a light rose-colored skirt and top with a beautiful silk floral printed scarf. It took days to find such simplicity. But at least that part of it was taken care of.

My dress, on the other hand, I had found at Casual Corner. It was just "weddingy" looking enough. I didn't want to go full-tilt bridal because my fiancé had been married before. It was a gorgeous dress. It was off-white underneath, had a sweetheart neckline, and had lace sleeves and lace over the satin on the neckline. It was the eighties so of course it had shoulder pads. The back was the most beautiful part of the dress. It had a keyhole back in the lace and a small satin bustle. It was cocktail length and absolutely stunning. It fit me like a glove. I showed it to my mom, and she thought it was pretty but asked me to go get it in a bigger size so I could have it tailored at her friend's bridal shop. I told her I didn't think that was necessary, but she made a good case for a custom fit. So I went and exchanged it for one size up. The following week I made an appointment at her friend's bridal store. I had met Mom's friend before. She was a really nice, funny woman. I liked her. She was very excited that I was getting married. She introduced me to the dressmaker. I put on the dress for her, and she pinned and pinned and pinned. She didn't do a lot of talking. I took the dress off and left it behind to be custom fit. I was told to come back in two weeks for another fitting. So a couple weeks went by and a friend of mine came with me to the fitting. I looked at the dress and instantly realized something looked wrong. I put it on and found there were about twenty to thirty satin-covered buttons that closed the keyhole back shut. The dressmaker came in and asked me how I liked it. I asked her who told her she could put these buttons on the opening of the back of my dress. She told me I couldn't walk down the aisle with my back showing. I replied, "Says who?" I was so angry. I continued to explain to her that for me, the beauty of the dress was the keyhole back. I told her she better be able to get all those buttons off without ruining the dress or she would buy me a new one. She looked shocked at my reaction. Who does that? What tailor, seamstress, or dressmaker makes a major decision like that without consulting the person that owns the garment? I left the dress with her and walked out. When I went back a couple weeks later, the dress was back to the way it SHOULD'VE been and SHOULD'VE stayed!

Flash-forward to just a couple years ago, I was telling one of my close girlfriends about the dress incident. This particular girlfriend has clothes tailored all of the time. She said she had never heard of any tailor taking on that kind of extra work without being told to do so. I know I didn't tell her to do it. Should we speculate who called her friend that owned the bridal shop? I can. I have no proof my mother did this because the woman that owned the shop died years ago, and the shop closed even before she died. I'm left to wonder. But my three closest friends agree this sounded like something my mom would have done. How it never crossed my mind at the time, I don't know. Maybe it SHOULD have.

We had our wedding reception at a country club. Before the dress incident, my mom and I went out to the country club to talk to the caterer. He was such a nice guy and did his job well. He presented us with many options: per-plate dinners, buffet style, appetizers. I told him what I thought would be good to serve from the kitchen, as opposed to a buffet. My mom decided it was going to be a buffet. She wouldn't let me get a word in edgewise. It was actually more like her wedding, her choices. It was all so frustrating. I stopped talking. I totally shut down. She signed all the agreements with the caterer, and we drove home. I talked to my fiancé about how she had belittled and humiliated me by talking down to me regarding anything I wanted for the reception. Remember, my fiancé didn't want to be involved. The only thing he wanted was an open bar and a small boutonniere for his suit jacket. Otherwise everything else was up to me. I asked him how he felt about a very small wedding and reception. He was fine with it.

The next day I called the caterer and canceled everything. My fiancé and I started talking about a much smaller venue and a party later on. I really had had enough…I thought. I talked to my mom the next day and told her I had canceled everything, and my fiancé and I were going to do this on our own without so much drama. If I recall, she hung up on me. A few hours later, my father showed up at our door. He had our wedding invitations in his hand. He came in, sat down, and begged me to please not cancel everything. He really wanted the honor of walking me down the aisle. He promised to "manage" my mother. I told him I wasn't sure if I wanted the hassle of all of this anymore. It was just too much fighting for me. I don't know how long he sat there and waited, but I finally acquiesced. My dad was a salesman. He was working the most difficult sales pitch of his life. I SHOULD'VE known better. So the next day I called the caterer and ordered the food I wanted…buffet style. I know…

My mother wrote a cake-decorating magazine from the time I was a little girl. I have seen all kinds of cakes, especially wedding cakes. There would be no other place I would go to have my wedding cake done. The company my mother worked for did the most beautiful cakes. I had spent lots of time there. All the people in my mom's office were so excited that I was getting married. I knew the woman who designed and made the wedding cakes. I met with her to discuss what my vision was. Of course my mom was there too… ever-present. I started to describe a cake I had seen in the magazine. It was a little less traditional for back then. I wanted rectangular cakes that "stepped up" like a staircase. Just four graduated sizes. I was asking the decorator advice on flavors and icings. In my mind's eye it was perfect and unique. All of a sudden my mom says, "That's the dumbest thing I've ever heard. That's not going to happen." I went blank, and I totally shut down. My mom continued to talk to the cake decorator about what she wanted. I realized I could hardly hear anything. It was like someone turned the volume down on the TV and stuffed my ears with cotton. I felt disoriented. I "came back" from whatever that was and heard the decorator say, "And then there will be chocolate filigree wings on each tier." Not stair steps, tiers, like a "typical" everyone else's wedding cake. The decorator said, "Doesn't that sound beautiful?" I nodded and left. Obviously this was not my wedding. It was hijacked by my mother.

I hired a well-known local band for the reception. The keyboard player was a good friend of mine. I asked him if he would be willing to play without his band for the cocktail hour at the reception. He agreed. I was happy he was going to be there and happy he was going to make money. What I wasn't happy with was before the cocktail hour started, my mother was being exceptionally rude to him. I went over and apologized to him. I told him she had been difficult at best during this whole wedding process. I'm so glad he didn't blame me, or worse yet leave and take his band with him.

Many years later, after I had gotten married, I was over at her house, and we were standing in her driveway. She started talking to me about kids. I think I had been married a little over a year. She started trying to "sell" me on the idea of having a child. "Sell" is a little light. Guilt me into having a baby is more accurate. Mind you, my sister had two kids, so she already had grandchildren. She said to me, a child from me would be the most special child ever. No child would ever be loved more. I thought that was odd because she already had grandchildren that she loved a lot. It struck me as the "most wanted baby in America" thing she had told me about myself. It did feel she was turning up the pressure a bit. I was twenty-eight at the time. After growing up in the abusive atmosphere, not just the guilt, the shaming, the belittling, I'm talking about the physical abuse, I had decided not to have children. I wasn't 100 percent sure I could break the cycle of violence. I wouldn't want to put a child through what I went through. I had done a lot of reading and research. There was nothing that would guarantee I would be able to stop myself from perpetuating violence. It scared me. But again, I was afraid of everything, all of the time. Are we sensing a theme? What I didn't realize was that I was so aware of my background, it would have prevented me from being that way. I'll get into that in another chapter.

Many years later, Mom got sick again. This time it wasn't non-Hodgkin's lymphoma, it was myelodysplastic syndrome (most recently brought to light by Robin Roberts on *Good Morning America*). From what I understood the doctors told us it had to do with the chemo that Mom had had. What happened was the myelodysplasia turned into acute leukemia after some time. I'm a little hazy on how long that took. My parents vacationed every year in Palm Springs, California. Their last trip Mom had to be air-ambulanced back here. She had a bunch of tests that concluded she had acute leukemia, and the family was told she only had three weeks to live. She left the hospital and came home. There were lots of people coming around to visit. We all took turns sitting with her so others could get out. The dysfunction of my family was really apparent by now. I was married, and my then-husband was not supportive of me spending time at my parents' house. He wanted me to do what he wanted me to do. My dad and sister made it clear that I couldn't handle any of what was going on or about to happen. So much negativity. It did undermine whatever confidence in myself I had. In fact, I hired a friend of mine who was a nurse to sit with me when it was my turn to be with my mother. I was sure if Mom died on "my watch," everyone would blame me. Not leukemia…me. I was terrified. But again, I was afraid everything all of the time. She died March 6, 1994, two days after my parents' forty-ninth wedding anniversary.

A couple of months before my mom died, she took me to her office. She sat me down with her boss and told me I had to take over writing the cake-decorating magazine. It wasn't something I really wanted to do, but I thought I SHOULD to preserve my mother's legacy. I had my own career as a manicurist. I had my own life. But I was willing to give it all up to preserve her legacy. There I was, "SHOULDING on myself" again. But I never took over for her. In fact, the owners didn't ask me to. The magazine folded, as did the business a couple of years after Mom died. The company wrote a beautiful tribute column about my mom. And that was that.

Two days before Mom died, she and I had our last conversation. My dad called early morning on March 4 saying, "Your mother is coughing up buckets of blood." My then-husband and I drove to my mom's. I walked into her room, and she was lying there with a glassy look in her eyes. She had blood on her fingers and her chin. I said, "Hi. What are you doing scaring us this way?" She sort of tried to smile and stared at me. I went into the bathroom and got two washcloths, one with soap and warm water, one was dry. I sat down on the bed with her and proceeded to clean the blood off of her. I was thinking Mom was vain about her appearance. She wouldn't have wanted anyone to see her that way. She said, "I feel so sorry for you." I asked her, "How many times did you clean up my skinned knees?" She smiled. "And how many times did you hold my hair back when

I was throwing up?" She smiled. "And whose mother would go find buckets of water to clean up the parking lot when I threw up on the doctor's office parking lot?" She tried to laugh. She said, "But you are my baby." And I said, "Why don't you let me do this, and you be my baby now." Nothing else was said. That was my last conversation with her. She died two days later. I got a call from my dad March 6, and he said, "She's gone." He had gone to take a shower and when he went to check on her she had passed.

When I got there, she was still warm. My aunt (my mom's sister) saw the look in my eyes and said to me, "Let's say the Shema." The Shema is a Jewish prayer, which is the centerpiece of all Jewish prayers. It was a wonderful thing for her to do. I needed some direction. It was perfect. I will always be grateful to her for that.

Now that I have written these things down and reread them, I realize there's a pattern with my mother. Whatever made me happy, be it dance, guitar, planning a wedding, she made sure to try and ruin it for me or at least take credit for what I had accomplished on my own. I will never know why she was that way. But because of the horrible relationship I had with my father, I figured I SHOULD love her twice as much. The truth is, neither of them could be trusted to keep me safe.

That was the big epiphany at age fifty-one. Not only was my mother complicit in my abuse, she generally set it up by getting my dad enraged. I didn't stand a chance...

CHAPTER 5

Sister

Can you imagine my sister's surprise to find out she wasn't going to be an only child? At age twelve, she was going to have to share her life with a new baby.

It was my understanding from books like <u>Little Women</u>, movies like *Mary Poppins,* and TV shows like *Leave it to Beaver*, that siblings were supposed to get along or that siblings form an automatic bond because they're blood. Little did I know what I would be in for. I now know that books, movies, and TV shows are for entertainment and are fictional.

I understand that twelve years is a long time. I've always said we are two only children from the same family. Pretty much my whole life I've tried to have a relationship with my sister. What I didn't realize until as recently as a year ago, it takes two. I knew it applied to couples, but didn't realize it wasn't an automatic thing to bond just because you were siblings and have grown up in the same atmosphere.

What I noticed from a really young age was my sister's disgust for me. She had no patience around me. She was always condescending and dismissive of me. But I kept trying to win her over. We certainly didn't "feel" like anything I had seen on TV.

One of my sister's favorite stories for years was to tell people when she was babysitting me she dropped me on my head. That must be what's wrong with me according to her. She thinks it's funny. Ha-ha...*Not!*

As I got older, I tried being helpful. If she was sick, I would bring her groceries. One particular time I picked up a couple of bags of groceries for her. I called her from her apartment lobby and asked her to meet me at the elevator. At the time I was terrified of elevators. So I put the groceries in the elevator and ran up the stairs. I stepped out of the stairwell and the elevator was just opening. My sister was in the hallway, and all she could say was, "This isn't very convenient, you know." Not thank you. But I persevered. I would babysit her kids. If she went out of town I would stay at her house to take care of my niece and nephew. No real heartfelt thank-yous were given, just an expectation of me being able to help her. That was fine if we were going to bond like sisters SHOULD. There's that word again. I don't know why I wasn't catching a clue that a sisterly relationship was probably never going to happen.

When I was fifteen, I contracted mono. Every year my parents went to Palm Springs for a month or more for vacation. That year I was so sick, but my parents decided to go anyway leaving me with my sister and her first husband to take care of me. They moved into my parents' house. When they pulled up into the driveway, they got out of their car and came inside. The first thing my sister said was, "Go out and get our bags." What? Not wanting to cause myself any problems I went out and dragged in their luggage. Then she told me to fix dinner. Now really, who would want someone with mono cooking for them? After dinner I was sitting on the floor wrapping presents, and my sister told me to clean up what I was doing. I told her I was almost done. She started yelling, walked over, and started hitting me in the face and head. I grabbed her hand and dug my fingernails into the back of her hand until she was bleeding. I just wanted her to stop hitting me. She knew better! She didn't like it when Dad hit her. None of it made any sense to me. But what happened next was mind-blowing. Her husband ran over, hit me, and said, "Look what you've done to your sister!" These were the people who were supposed to take care of me. These were the people I was supposed to rely on? How was I going to get well? What was I supposed to do? I can honestly say I don't remember much else. I just know that a few days later, the doctor said I had a case of hepatitis that went along with having severe mono. The doctor called my parents in Palm Springs and told them it would be a good idea to fly me out there to get some sun and rest. Again, I don't remember much. But I do remember my grandfather running up to me as I deplaned in Palm Springs. He said I was "milk white" and he thought I was going to faint.

I remember being at my mom's house sitting on the front steps. I was probably twenty-three. My sister came over, and we were all talking. I couldn't tell you what we were talking about. We got up to go in the house, and my sister brushed by me and said, "You know, I don't approve of your life." I had no idea where that came from. Furthermore, I never asked her to approve of my life. That stands out as a lightning-bolt moment for me. That was my realization that we would never be sisterly or bonded. But SHOULDN'T we? We were both getting older, but there was a tone of condescension in her voice, such judgment. Maybe I needed to be a little older to understand? But that moment would be prominent in my thoughts every time we would speak from that day forward.

Another confusing time for me with my sister was in 1987, the night I got home from my honeymoon. My then-husband and I had just gone to bed around eleven thirty, and the phone rang. It was my sister. She said, "Your niece is drunk and has been thrown out of a moving car. She's covered in mud." I asked if she needed me to come over. She said yes. So I got up, got dressed, and drove to her apartment. There was my niece sitting on the floor making what I called "exorcist noises." She clearly was hammered. Her long brown hair was caked with mud. She didn't seem to be hurt, bruised or bloody, just a mess. My sister launched into an "I just didn't know what to do" tirade. She kept mentioning her boyfriend. She had been long divorced at that time. She kept saying how this had ruined her date, and he was going to be so mad at her. He may not want to go out with her anymore. This was all she was concerned about. I picked my niece up off the floor and helped her into the bathroom. I took her muddy clothes off and got in the shower with her (fully dressed). I washed her hair and got the mud off of her. I dried her off, wrapped her in a towel, and sat her in the rocking chair. Unfortunately, she rocked herself out of the chair and into a crumpled heap on the floor. While this was happening, my sister was still going on and on about her boyfriend. I finally told her to leave the room and go to sleep. I just couldn't believe what her priorities seemed to be. A little askew I would say. I got a dry, clean T-shirt from my sister and planned to stay awhile. I really wanted to keep my niece sitting up and awake. After an hour or so I finally put her to bed. The only all-night programming back then was roller derby. So I sat up all night watching roller derby and every twenty minutes made sure my niece was breathing. About 7:00 a.m. I decided to go home with my souvenir "Welcome to Jamaica" T-shirt. I never gave it back. You know the saying "My sister called, my niece was drunk and thrown from a moving car, and all I got was this lousy T-shirt…"

My Family—The Fowl Experience

Over the years my sister and I have gotten together for family dinners. I would call them family functions but that would be a misnomer. For years I've cooked and transported the turkey for Thanksgiving. This particular year, Thanksgiving was at my sister and her fiancé's house. I was told to be there at six thirty. So I timed the roasting and resting of the turkey for that time. I spent my day off trying to relax. At two thirty I got a call from my sister saying she wanted a hot turkey served. I told her you don't serve hot turkey because it won't slice right. You need it to rest a bit and cool off. She started yelling she wanted hot turkey. Again, the theme with my sister. Not wanting to cause any problems, I would bring a hot turkey. Transporting a twenty-five-pound hot turkey, juices sloshing, was going to be a trick. So at five thirty I put the turkey back in the oven. At six o'clock my sister called and said, "Where are you?" I reminded her she had called me at home. She wanted to know why I wasn't there. I reminded her she told me six thirty. She started screaming at me about how wrong I was. I could hear people in the background. Clearly her guests were already there. She said she wanted me there now! I again reminded her she wanted a hot turkey and that the turkey was in the oven. She asked me when I was going to be there. I said six thirty, like she told me. She hung up on me. Now what I'm about to reveal, only my closest friends know. The following wasn't an afterthought or even 20-20 hindsight. I stood in my kitchen, the turkey in front of me. I thought, if I cut off a turkey breast I could keep that and have Thanksgiving by myself. I could call a cab and send the rest of the turkey in the backseat and pay half the cab fare. Send the turkey to my sister's house and have the driver hold the turkey "hostage" until the rest of the fare was paid. I went back and forth, back and forth weighing the consequences. On one hand it was really funny to me and would have made quite a statement. On the other hand, there would be such a backlash, and my family would make me miserable for the rest of my life. As I look back at it now, they were already pretty miserable to me so I probably SHOULD have gone ahead and done it. But no, I was too afraid. I just didn't want to deal with the consequences.

So I brought the turkey, hot, sloshing juices and all to her house. I walked in and put the turkey on the table and joined the other guests. My sister walked up to me in a very stern voice and said, "Where is the turkey?" I told her to turn around and look at the foil-topped pan on the table. She rolled her eyes and walked away. I went on socializing mostly with my sister's stepson and his girlfriend. This was the girlfriend's first Thanksgiving with everyone. She was (and is) so lovely, charming and funny. It came time for all of us to sit down at the beautifully set dining room table. I think there were fifteen or sixteen of us. I was seated across from the stepson and his girlfriend. My sister realized she was one place setting short. My stepmother said, "That's OK, we'll just slide over." My sister started repeating over and over again, "But I counted, but I counted." She was looking around and literally pointed right at the new girlfriend and says, "Oh, I didn't count you." Well, the three of us couldn't even look at each other. We were trying so hard not to laugh. It was just so shockingly rude! Again, my stepmother suggested we slide over and my sister said, "No, I'll just eat in the kitchen." Unbelievable. We finally convinced her to set another place at the table. Dinner went on, but the girlfriend, stepson, and I could barely look at each other all night. That wasn't stressful, not at all.

The most ridiculous and painful things happened because of family gatherings. I can recall so many hurtful, embarrassing things that happened starting from when I was a child up until just recently.

Keeping with the sister theme, in 2011 my sister invited the family to her house for dinner. My niece, her husband, and their kids were here from out of town. I was really looking forward to seeing how much the kids had grown and also catching up with what my niece had been up to. I was on my way over to pick up my dad and his wife when my cell phone rang. It was my sister. She said, "I don't think I cooked anything you can eat." Now to tell you the truth, this didn't surprise me. But really who does that? As usual this made it appear that something else was my fault. Now it was somehow picky eating. The first thing I said was, "What do you want me to do? Put a chicken in my purse?" She became miffed by my attitude. Before she could say anything else I asked, "Is there salad?" She said there was. I replied, "Then there's something I can eat."

When we arrived the kids were sitting at the table eating spa-ghetti noodles with butter and bread. In the sink there was a colander full of noodles. As we settled into eat, I asked if I could have some noodles. My sister yelled to my niece, "Could Roberta have some noodles or will the kids want seconds?" My niece said of course I could, and the kids wouldn't want any more. So I put some noodles on my plate and put the plate in the microwave. Unfortunately she had a microwave that you need to be a rocket scientist to work. I stood there reading the different buttons. The next thing I knew I was shoulder blocked out of the way by my sister and in her most condescending and bitter tone said, "Oh just let me do it." Begging the question, why do I go to these things? After that tension-filled meal, I was glad to go home. Again, why do I go in the first place? Because, for some reason I think I SHOULD. I SHOULD spend time with my elderly father. I SHOULD spend time with my fam-ily, however dysfunctional it may be. After much contemplation, I determined I was just afraid. Afraid of rocking the boat, afraid of people being mad, afraid of emotional maybe even physical abuse.

All I know is that I didn't come away from family events feeling good or healthy. Just exhausted and mentally drained.

My sister thinks she saved me from being obese. My parents had a rule about "the clean-plate club." If I didn't finish what was dished out for me, I was grounded. The same must have been true for my sister. When I was around nine or ten my sister said to my dad, "Do you want her to be obese? That's what will happen if you make her clean her plate." I don't know how, but he realized he'd rather have me thin than fat. The truth is, I would've been grounded rather than eat something I didn't want to eat, hence, being grounded after almost every dinner until I was nine.

One night my mom made cocktail weenies in barbecue sauce. I was not a fan at all. I ate one and didn't like it. I was told I couldn't go to my friend's house for a sleepover if I didn't finish every last one of those cocktail weenies. I sat there staring at them. I weighed out what was more important. Not eating those awful things or losing a sleepover. I sat there going back and forth, trying to decide. I sat there while they cleared the table with the exception of my plate. I must've sat there over an hour. I finally decided I would suck it up and eat them. I ate them all, as cold and awful as they were. I finished, cleaned my plate, got my sleepover stuff, and was going to head out the door to the neighbor's house. My dad stopped me and told me I wasn't going anywhere. But I finished all the food on my plate. I SHOULD be able to go. He told me I couldn't go because I had waited too long to eat my dinner, and I was grounded. What? I ate those awful things for nothing? He told me next time I would make my mind up sooner. So into my room I went. Again afraid, off-kilter, disbelieving. How did one play the game around my family? Nothing made sense. What I was realizing was you can't play the game if the rules keep changing.

I have to say up to this point my sister and I have had a loving moment or two. Not enough to fill even one page. My mother was dying of cancer in 1994. My anxiety disorder was rearing its ugly head, but I did my best to be there by my mom's side. A couple days before she died, my sister took me aside and said, "I can't even imagine how you are gauging this." She was speaking of my anxiety disorder and how anxious she was feeling through this process. Ah, a moment of support! She asked my then-husband not to go on his business trip because things were near the end with my mom. After they bickered back and forth, he relented and stayed in town. So pretty much there they are, the moments of support. Even when my dad died, she wasn't very helpful to me. No sisterly connection, some discussion, no connection and lots of judgment.

In 1988, my then husband and I were giving a Chanukah party at our house. Friends and family were invited. I got a call from my sister telling me she wanted to bring four of her friends with her. I told her we didn't really have the seating space. She told me she wouldn't come unless she could bring these people. I knew if she didn't come it would upset our parents, and I'd never hear the end of it. So we squeezed everyone in.

In 2000, my sister decided to have Thanksgiving at her house. I was long divorced by then. I asked if I could bring my best friend and her husband with me. They were in town for just a few days. She said no. I asked her one more time. She again said no. So my friend and I had our own peaceful Thanksgiving. The best part of not being there was hearing from my stepmother the next day. Evidently my brother-in-law tried a new recipe he found online that said you can cook a fifteen- to twenty-pound turkey in a convection oven in an hour. Well, it didn't work out so well. The turkey wasn't served until after 8:00 p.m. So glad I got to miss out on the drama of that "family gathering."

Our mom died March 6, 1994. Passover was three or four weeks after that. This would be our first Passover without Mom. The week before she died, I was sitting with her, and she asked me if I knew how to make "the soup." I knew she was referring to the big stockpot full of chicken soup with matzo balls for Passover. She told me the recipe and said she had a secret ingredient but I SHOULDN'T tell anyone—and by the way, I never have. So of course it was up to me to make the soup for Passover. Even though I was doing the majority of the cooking, Passover was going to be at Dad's house. As I was making the soup in that same stockpot my mom had used, I was standing in my own kitchen cooking, crying and definitely feeling the pressure of the legacy of "the soup." Cook, cry, stir. I dragged all the food to Dad's house and set the table. We all sat down for our first Seder without Mom. It was surreal. After the Seder service it was time to dish out the soup. In our family there are the "ladlers" and there are "runners." I was now the "ladler," and my sister, one of the "runners." As I dished the first bowl my sister said, "That's not Mom's soup!" I told her it most certainly was. She replied, "You didn't strain it through cheesecloth. Does that look like Mom's soup?" I told her Mom never said anything to me about cheesecloth. She said, "Well, Mom's soup didn't have anything floating in it, hers was clear broth." I was devastated. It was already hard enough, but to be scolded about what I SHOULD have done and what I SHOULD have known? I could hardly breathe. On top of which she was belittling me in front of everyone. I didn't hear her volunteering to make the soup or much of anything, for that matter. By the way, no one else complained about herbs "floating" in the soup. And I can honestly say I found my own recipe for chicken soup and my own "recipe" for not pressuring myself, especially on holidays.

As long as we're on the subject of judgment, I might as well tackle some of the more interesting/hurtful judgmental instances. I do know there's a difference between having an opinion (you know opinions are like assholes, everybody's got one) and judgment. Several months before my dad died, I was on the phone with my sister. I was sitting in my home office, and we got into a lengthy but general conversation. The conversation all of a sudden took a turn into finances. My finances, to be exact. I don't even know where it came from. All I know is I was being judged for how I worked, how much money I spent, and what my financial priorities should be. I couldn't believe it because I didn't discuss the specifics of my financial life with her. What did she know? I kept asking her, then yelling at her to stop judging me. Then it turned into a free-for-all. I started talking about when Dad dies, we're it. We are the blood relatives left in the state. I heard myself practically begging her to be my sister. I was crying. But more than the memory of the emotion, I remember being totally focused on the back step of the townhouse across the courtyard. I was just staring at it. The deck attached to the stairs. I felt out of body. I'm sure it was a PTSD reaction. I heard myself say, "Once Dad is gone, you're going to find a reason not to have anything to do with me." And that is exactly what has happened. We haven't spoken since October 2013, and I don't expect we will. Our last conversation was regarding MNSure, Minnesota's answer to the Affordable Health Care Act. She wanted to help me sign up. Obviously she didn't think I could do it on my own. She wanted to come over and help me. I told her I would take care of it on my own. I got off the phone and sat there thinking that her opinion of me wasn't really any different than my father's or mother's. I waited a day and decided to send her an e-mail explaining her how I felt. Our last exchanges were e-mails as follows:

> I spent some time thinking about what to say to you. When you called yesterday to offer me your "help" with signing up for MNSure, I didn't know what to say. So I didn't say much of anything. But now that I've had a chance to think about it, I find your suggestion to come over and "help" intrusive, insulting and just plain condescending. What would make you think I would need your help, or that I would want to share any of my personal information with you? You haven't exactly been "helpful" to me in the past. If you are so fascinated by MNSure, go online and read about it. FYI: The site was still down this morning. It's up and running now. I've even taken care of everything all by myself!!
>
> Roberta

> *I'm on a break at work so this will be quick. As usual you misconstrued what I was saying/asking and of course your way is always and only the right way. If I wanted to do as you said here. I would have called*

you a dummy who could never figure it out on your own and then I would know all your secret information and use it against you. You wear me out.

What I think is even more interesting is that it never crossed my mind you would get my "secret information and use it against" me. I think what's wearing you out is that I won't take what you say to me at face value anymore.

Roberta

No…what's wearing me out is your paranoia about me and my motives. As I said, I had none of the thoughts you ascribed to me. I'm finished walking on egg shells with you. If that's your need, to examine every word that comes out of my mouth, go ahead and use your energy to do that. But for me, enough.

So with the words, "But for me, enough," I realized I SHOULD have been done years ago. Would I prefer that we were speaking? Sure. Would I prefer we were a "bonded sisterly unit"? Absolutely. But wishing won't make it so. Any amount of work or effort I've made in the past has just gotten more judgment and condescension from her. She's very much like our mother in her need for material things and having the last word. She's very much like our father in her self-involvement, narcissism, and her condescension and dismissiveness of me. So she got the last word and what she wanted. After Dad died she found a way to have nothing to do with me. And for the first time in my life, I'm OK with that. It's actually pretty freeing, as it SHOULD be. I did send her an e-mail on her birthday with an emoticon of the cake. I didn't feel it warranted more attention than that. She sent me a card for my birthday. At that time the one-year anniversary of my dad's death was looming. I wasn't sure how I felt about it. As I said in the opening of the book, the irony didn't escape me that I started to write a year to the day after his death. My dad's Yahrzeit was the weekend of January 10 to 12, 2014. That would be one Friday night service and two short fifteen-minute services on Saturday and Sunday. On January 9, I received an e-mail from my sister, subject line: "Letting you know." "Just wanted you to know we are bringing [stepmother] to the six o'clock Saturday evening service at Temple." That's it. That's all it said. I couldn't decide if it was a warning, a shot across the bow, if you will, or was it an, "if you'd like to see us that's when we'll be there." My impression, it was a warning. It certainly was no invitation. I had been struggling with whether I wanted to attend the service and honor my father at all. As it happened, I did not go to any of the services. I didn't go to my mother's a month later either. That was the first time in twenty-one years. Those decisions I made in 2014 don't have to be permanent, I just have to honor my own feelings first.

So you would think that this chapter about my sister would be done. How could there be more? We aren't speaking. Well, in my family even that doesn't stop strange things from happening, but that's another story that's in another chapter. Because we are not speaking, that means I'm hearing nothing about my niece and her family or my nephew. I had a strong feeling I should call my niece. I do have to add at this point my niece and nephew are not great at getting back to people. It's nothing personal, just the way it is. I called my niece on a Wednesday and left a message saying I just wanted to say hi and see how everything was and hoped everything was OK. I hadn't heard back by Friday, so I texted her and said, "Left you a message on Wednesday, hope everything is OK." I got a text back within a few minutes that said, "Hi! Just starting to be able to talk and focus. Thank you for the message! I'm good, healing. They got all the cancer, so I'm very happy." What? I texted back "Cancer…I know nothing. I'm calling, answer your phone." She texted back, "Sure."

So I called, and we talked. I said, "What cancer?" She said, "You know I had thyroid cancer." A couple of years ago, yeah. "Well they had to take some lymph nodes out. I'm going to be fine." I had spoken to her months before and told her that her mother and I were not speaking, so I'm out of the loop. She said to me, "Maybe it would be worth keeping in touch with mom so you know these things." I said it would be worth keeping in touch with her so I would know these things, and she SHOULD probably stay out of the middle.

My conclusion after speaking to my niece was that it was a much more important message via e-mail to let me know my sister was bringing the stepmother to Temple than it was for me to know via e-mail my niece was having cancer surgery. All I could do was shake my head in disbelief.

I have spent a lifetime trying to have a relationship with my sister and that same lifetime trying to understand her and her motivation. I would think of it as wasted time, but the "glass half full" side of me knows this last round has taught me a lot about myself and what behavior I will and won't tolerate in my life.

CHAPTER 6

Me

So I thought I would write about my expectations of having a "family." I don't know where my expectations came from, they were just there. Maybe better put what I thought a family SHOULD be. For as long as I can remember, I thought a family was who you lived with, who loved you unconditionally and supported your dreams, ambitions, and aspirations. Is this a Pollyanna view? I didn't think so. I always operated with the notion that my family would be those people, even if it was shown to me to be otherwise. I don't think my belief in unconditional love and acceptance wavered. Whatever physical or emotional abuse happened, I still believed that "my family" would be there for me no matter what. It has become clear to me after writing for so many months about living and dealing with my so-called family, that that was never the case.

Recently I was talking to my therapist and asking him how I couldn't see this sooner. As I said, I started understanding what happened throughout my life with "my family" when I was fifty-one. And even then it was just the tip of the iceberg. He told me I had to believe what I was thinking, that they were there for me because I had no choice. And then my therapist said something that made my heart sink and made me sick to my stomach. A bombshell "Aha moment." He said, "Even abused dogs look to their abusers to feed them and take care of them." UGH! It took my breath away. That statement alone was like a gut punch. It makes me sad, it makes me uncomfortable, and it speaks volumes!

No matter what happened I expected a cohesive family unit somehow. But it was never to be. It's a good thing I didn't realize it at the time. What would I have done?

At fifty-five my new job in life is to find myself and find my joy. I've never been an "oh, woe is me" kind of person. The glass has been mostly half full throughout. But I now realize I have been holding myself back. I held my emotions back by keeping myself in the middle ground. Not too high, not too low, just in the middle. Kind of sounds like the three bears. And I realize now that there is no joy in that. It's mere existence. Again, I'm not unhappy, just not unleashed. Now the search begins for my joy.

I always loved music. I don't know if my love is like other people's. I love songs for how they make me feel and what memories, when I hear them, the music evokes, good or bad. Music always elicits a response from me. But my love of music includes the progression of the actual notes. How one note steps up or down to another, tone quality, clever phrasing. It's always been that way. When I think of songs or sing a cappella, the songs are fully orchestrated in my head. I used to worry about that. What did it mean that I heard fully orchestrated songs when no music was playing? I've come to terms with the fact it's just the way I'm wired. Recently I found out Lionel Richie hears fully orchestrated music in his head too. I'm in good company.

So armed with all that knowledge, I decided to take voice lessons. I always loved to sing but had been stifled by my family or in one case when I was in my twenties, a local music producer. He told me if I didn't get rid of my vibrato, my singing career wouldn't go anywhere. I don't think my goal was to ever have a singing career. But each of the criticisms I encountered stopped me from singing for periods of time. But I knew I loved singing. Then came the era of karaoke. Oh how I wanted to sing! So I started going to a local club, and there I sat too terrified to sing. It took me an entire year of watching and listening before I got up on stage and sang a duet with someone. Sonny and Cher's "I've Got You Babe." I shook while I sang, but I was doing it. Now you can't pry that microphone out of my cold dead hand. I've been singing at karaoke places for fifteen years. I'm still nervous every time I get up to walk to the stage, but I still do it. I can tell you I don't think I sing full out, and I'm never satisfied with how I sound. I always find fault. No one else does, just me.

Back to singing lessons. I got a booklet regarding community education, and there was a voice-lesson class listed. I decided now was the time. I was going to explore my voice, learn the ins and outs, what my voice would and would not support. After a couple of weeks, I signed up for class. The instructor was wonderful. She taught us a lot about breath control, tone quality, and adjustments. She taught me about what I called my falsetto. It's actually called a "whistle register." So much to learn. The first week the students and instructor didn't do much singing. We did do voice warm-up exercises and sang scales. Our homework assignment was to pick a song to sing in class that we could work on for the next few weeks. So many songs, so many choices. My first thought was to sing something I always sing when I'm at karaoke. Nope, not going to do that. Pick something meaningful and emotional. Nope, I don't need to break down crying in class. Pick something that runs my entire range. Nope. Pick something unexpected that I would never sing at karaoke. Something that I love. Show tunes! *Guys and Dolls.* My favorite, especially when I'm listening to the original Broadway soundtrack. "If I Were a Bell" was my choice. It was fun, animated, and in my "whistle register" where I love to sing. I practiced all week and was sure it was the right choice...until an hour and a half before class. Nerves got the best of me. But I went with it anyway. I got to class and was a little shaky. The time arrived for me to sing. The two guys in my class chose me to go first. I think in show business it's called "flop sweat." I sang, I hit all the notes, my breath control was good...surprisingly. My hands were sweating, and it was a very long three minutes. I got done, took a deep breath, and waited for the criticism. There wasn't any. The instructor had me play with the tone in my voice when I sang it for the second time. I knew I had to learn to let go and enjoy myself. So now I had to work on that. The last class there were only two students left—myself and a gentleman about my age. This was our week to shine with our respective songs. This time I told him to go first. He was much improved from the second week. I was hoping I was too. It was my turn, and I decided to try to let go a bit. I had more fun but still something was holding me back. The instructor told me I had a lot of voice and knew there was much more. She said she had a feeling I wanted to break out and let loose but wasn't allowing myself to do it. She asked me why did I think I did that? I felt my breath seize up a bit, and I felt tears coming. What was going on? I decided to be honest with my answer and pay the consequences of crying. I told her when I sing in front of people it's like looking in a mirror. I can see myself, and I feel really vulnerable and exposed. I could hear my inner critics say, "That was a sharp note." She assured me I wasn't singing sharp notes or flat notes. I told her my singing is really personal for me. Sharing it opens me up for criticism, at least that's the vulnerable part. She asked me to sing it again and stamp my feet, open my arms, and act it out. That really scared me. But I was game! I sang, I stomped, I projected, I acted a little. It was almost fun. She said she thought I was still holding back. Again she asked why. So with all the courage I could muster, I told her if I sang full out with abandon, it would be like bragging or showing off. I wouldn't want to do that, and then I started to cry. She shared that in her family, even though she sang and performed with them by the time she was six, her folks told her not to get a big head. In that moment I knew she understood. She was a nurturer. I also knew I would keep her in my life. I'm taking private lessons from her now that the community education class is over. Together we are going to help me find my voice and my joy!

The lesson I wish I knew how to teach: I wish I could make young people who grew up in the type of stifling atmosphere I grew up in see their value and understand that the messages they are being given by others don't necessarily line up with how you view yourself. I knew I was a good person. I knew I had friends. I knew I had talent. But unfortunately, the messages I was given continuously by my family were: I couldn't get along with anyone, I was stupid, careless, and lazy. I wish I could have filtered out all of the negativity and untruth. It took me years of therapy and practice, practice, practice to stop playing those old tapes. Even now, knowing better, a snippet of an old tape will play. I have to stop and ask myself where that came from and why. It usually has to do with some anxiety, however small, I'm feeling. But I really do know the truth. I am a good person. I am smart. I have long-term great friendships that mean the world to me. Those people see me for who I truly am. Those are the things that matter most to me.

—————— CHAPTER 6A ——————

Checking in with Myself

I've been writing this book for about two months. I usually write on the weekends because I'm so busy with work, and I can't afford to be distracted or upset while working. Today, March 14, 2014, I decided to check in with myself. I found myself particularly weepy. In fact, I've been weepy for a week or so. I've been asked if writing has been cathartic for me. The answer, not really. Maybe the better answer is, not yet. I'm looking forward to it eventually being cathartic. Right now it's just upsetting and painful. One more thing, it is clarifying. When I reread what I've written, I see a clear pattern of how my parents dealt with me. They did a lot of giving and taking away with the same hand and sometimes in the same breath. I was constantly off balance. That was done by word and by deed. The realization of how unsafe I was is now shockingly clear. I recently asked my therapist how I didn't see that growing up? He told me because I was living it day-to-day. I didn't know any different. I also didn't know that everyone's parents didn't act the same way when alone with their own kids. I hear quite often that there are no owner's manuals on how to raise kids. But you would think there SHOULD be common sense.

So again, to check in with myself is important. I know that there are days I don't want to write, but I do it anyway. There are days

I don't want to upset myself, but I write anyway. How does that song go? "Feelings, nothing more than feelings..." The impact of seeing the book come to fruition is deep. The writing is daunting. I know that I'm trying to save the "lighter stuff" to write down later. Maybe that will make it all worth it. I've told many people that writing the book will be good for me. Best-case scenario, number one: it will help someone going through the things I went through. Best-case scenario, number two: I'll publish this book, it will be well-received, and I'll make money off my crazy-ass family. In my fertile fantasy life, Oprah will call, telling me she's picked my book for her book club. I'll be able to meet her and maybe Tyler Perry too. Even Iyanla Vanzant will want to talk to me about my resiliency. Like I said, fertile fantasy life.

CHAPTER 7

Bullies and Betrayals

I think bullies can spot targets pretty quickly. In retrospect, I was a great target. My self-esteem was nearly nonexistent. I was afraid of so many different things. I just wanted to have friends, but I am sure the bullies could sense I would be easy to upset and gullible too. The neighborhood kids were tough to deal with. As I stated earlier, my first PTSD incident I can remember is because the neighborhood kids were pushing me down and trying to take my dress off. Why? At five years old I certainly didn't know why. The boys were crude and gross as boys will be when they are six to fourteen years old. Another time, I remember two of the boys taking out their penises and peeing into someone's bicycle handle. I think I was seven or eight. I think it was the first time I had seen a penis. They peed and laughed. I didn't understand why they were doing that and why it was funny.

As those boys got older, they got mean. They made up all kinds of names that were variations of my name like "Babitchca" and "Witchie Poo." It was upsetting and hurtful. But I kept trying to overcome. The girls, on the other hand, seemed to be my friends, at least on the surface. After years of being neighbors with one girl, she admitted she and the other neighbor kids would go into our house when we weren't there and steal stuff, mostly cookies and food. She also admitted she liked to be involved in getting me upset so they could see my parents get angry and yell at them. She also said they liked to get my parents upset with me so they could see my parents yell at me. But what they didn't know was what was going on behind closed doors. It wasn't exactly helpful with the amount of abuse that was going on. I spent a lot of time with those girls. I just wanted to have friends.

As we got older, we all moved away. A couple of us kept in touch. One woman became devoutly religious. When we got together at her father's memorial, she kept apologizing to me for how she treated me when we were growing up. I found out later if she apologized to me three times, she was absolved of her guilt and shame. It didn't matter if I forgave her. All she had to do was repeat her apology three times.

Her sister and I kept in touch maybe once a year. She had moved to the West Coast and would come back to her hometown and try to find the time to get together with her friends. She and I didn't really have a lot in common, but that wasn't a reason not to get together. The last time I saw her was when she was here in 2010. She had very specific plans for each one of her friends. She wanted to meet with me separately. She wanted to go with me to our old neighborhood. She wanted to go out to dinner. Then she wanted me to drop her off to see her cousins.

So she was dropped off at my apartment. I drove us over to our old neighborhood. We talked about a lot of different things. I was pretty candid about the abuse that had been going on in my house. I don't remember her having much of a reaction. I was surprised by that because she was a licensed social worker. I was perplexed by her schedule. But I went with it. We went to dinner. I remember feeling uncomfortable. She seemed a bit self-involved and not very warm and welcoming. Frankly, I was glad when dinner was over. We left the restaurant and got into my car. Honestly, there really was not a lot left to say. I pulled up to our (her) destination and was surprised when she asked me if I wanted to come in and see her cousins. I said sure, that would be nice. I walked in with her. I got a warm welcome. As one of her cousins started to ask me something, she said, "You can go now." I was kind of stunned by how blunt she was. I left and was relieved that my time with her was over. A month or two later I received the following e-mail from her. I kept it just as she sent it to me, typos and all; I just didn't include her name.

Hi Roberta,

These thoughts are my birthday gift to you.

1. It occurred to me that one reason you were teased and picked on a little kid was because you had no one else in your age cohort. A year was a big deal then. I wasn't friends with my sister's friends as they were in the same grade as her, not me. I was in the same grade as Mathew and then Cindy. You were in the same grade as Tommy B. but had no females in the neighborhood in your grade. I think that would have made a big difference. You were more or less alone as well as younger than us. (Our initial reason conscious was that you looked different than us. I'm sure, very cute to any adult, but to us you stood out as funny looking, with those high pig tails so easy to pull, and those bright wild clothes and tights your mom dressed you in.) But if you were in our grade or had someone else in your grade with you, I don't know if you would have been so scapegoated.

2. My other thought (hypothesis) is this: Although very cute to any adult, you were picked on initially because of your looks. I would have imagine that you developed an unconscious belief about not being safe in the world if you're not "pretty". Either you or your parents were aware of this and remedied it as you grew older: braces, nose job, nice clothes (that I was very envious of).

And it worked. You were liked, had friends, boys liked you and were attracted to you. Of course for more than your looks, but what I'm stressing is this unconscious belief of beauty=safety, lack of beauty=danger was reinforced (and your dad's magazines, I'm sure also fed into this). And so, why I bring this up is now that you're in menopause, I'm sure these unconscious beliefs will be surfacing. Everything that made you (feel) safe is leaving, and with that childhood experience around lack of beauty being dangerous, it would make complete and total sense if you started feeling more scared and afraid in the world without knowing why. Of course, these are just my thoughts—but I wanted to offer them to you as a birthday gift, just in case you've been feeling as such. (Part of why menopause is such Hell is that it brings up all our unconscious (-) beliefs and wounds; even those we thought we healed. - At least that's been my experience.)

Wishing you a year of great joy and a Happy (52nd) Birthday,

love,
[keeping her name anonymous]

I had to read it twice. I cried then got mad. But it hit me it wasn't my imagination that these kids were really mean to me. They were bullies. The other thing that occurred to me was in her point number two, she wasn't talking about me. She was talking about herself. What a nice "birthday gift." I haven't spoken to, e-mailed, or seen her since. I don't need to. She is yet another person who has assigned me a role she needs me to be in, but doesn't know me at all. More importantly, doesn't want to know me as I really am.

The Mean Girls

Yes, it is a movie. A movie I've never seen. Why? Because I knew the mean girls at school. If you ask anyone now who the mean girls were in school, everyone would say the same four to five girls' names. That in itself makes me feel better. It wasn't just me that thought these girls were awful. There were so many people who had the same kind of experiences I had. Even at our thirty-year high school reunion, nothing had changed with them. Amazing. In school these girls would belittle and humiliate others at every turn. Pointing and laughing. Again, I think that mean girls, like bullies, can spot a vulnerable target a mile away.

I remember in junior high one of those girls making fun of me while I was changing clothes for gym class. She was pointing and laughing with the other mean girls. Then the "pointer" came up to me and told me the way my crotch was sticking out she and the rest of the girls thought I was a man. Evidently my "mound" had developed before theirs did. That made for a fun time during gym class. Another time I was accused of wearing a padded bra. It was the mean girl who told us all if girls rubbed their breast area their boobs would grow. As we got into high school the mean girls became meaner. My life was already pretty difficult. This additional shit didn't help at all.

As I started therapy in my twenties, the "mean girls" subject was something I was trying to understand. My therapist suggested maybe I should call this particular woman that had really made my life miserable and tell her how I felt about it. That sounded reasonable. What could go wrong? I thought carefully about what I wanted to say. I waited a few days. I was trying to work up my courage. I made the call. She was gracious enough to listen to what I had to say. I told her that I thought we had been put into an unhealthy competition with each other by our parents. I brought up some things from junior high and high school. I wanted her to know that when I realized it wasn't about us, per se, I thought I SHOULD call her. I went on to say I didn't blame her for my misery. It was more about what my parents were doing. It was a nice conversation. She had some things she added. All was good when we hung up.

The ex-wife of my then-husband was friends with one of the mean girls. This ex-wife and I were very friendly. We spent a lot of time together. It was very adult. The ex-wife, the mean girl, and I all graduated from the same high school class. Our ten-year reunion was the year after I got married. The night of the reunion, my then-husband and I hired the sitter for the kids. We all went to the reunion. I realized that no one had changed that much in ten years. Cliques were still cliques. Mean girls were still mean. In fact, they wanted to start fights, physical and otherwise. I had to get out of there. So my then-husband and I left. The next day the ex-wife called and talked to my then husband. He said I SHOULD talk to her. So I did. Evidently, the mean girl that I had called years before for that heart-to-heart talk called her. She wanted to warn the ex-wife that I was sick and blamed her (the mean girl) for everything that had gone wrong in my life, and I was a danger to the kids. The first thing I remember was seeing my hair start to shake. I lowered my voice and said to the ex-wife, "You know better than to believe any of that. I would throw myself in front of a moving truck rather than let anything happen to your kids." I was furious she would have to check to see if any of that was true. We had been dealing with each other and spending time with each other for a couple of years by then. I went into a dark place in my head. I sat in the dark and didn't speak at home for two weeks. I would only lighten up when I was at work. Everything went back to normal when the ex-wife apologized. But can you imagine someone interjecting themselves that way? What for? To cause trouble, to belittle and humiliate me? Oh yeah, "mean girls"…high school…Some people just don't grow up. I look at it this way: some people peak in high school and have an inability to move forward or mature.

At the thirty-year reunion, the mean girls were together. Honestly, they weren't even very respectful of each other. It was kind of funny. Two of the mean girls were standing together watching me talk to the other ex-wife (by now I had been long divorced). I told you she and I liked each other, respected each other, with the exception of a couple of weeks after the ten-year reunion. We were standing together talking about the kids. The next thing I knew, these two "mean girls" walked up on either side of her and picked her up by her elbows and carried her off while she was in mid-sentence with me. It was laughable. She turned around as she was being carried off and mouthed the words, "I'm sorry." I waved to her and laughed. Some things never change.

One of my favorite things happened the night of our thirty-year reunion. This woman came up to me and started talking to me as if she knew me. I honestly had no idea who she was. She must have talked for a good three or four minutes when I finally stopped her and said, "I'm sorry, who are you?" She looked at me in disbelief. She told me her name. It was one of the mean girls! In fact, it was the pointer from gym class. I thought that was hysterical!

At that same reunion I ran into someone I really felt I needed to confront. Maybe confront is too harsh a word. But I certainly wanted to get something off my chest. This person has become a famous author. We all knew early on he was going to amount to something big. He wasn't a particularly nice kid, but he was smart. When I was at our ten-year high school reunion, I found him sitting on a window seat with his best friend from high school. I had covered up my name tag and walked up to say hi. Really, I didn't look that different. It had only been ten years. We started having a conversation. He stopped me and asked me who I was. I uncovered my name tag. He and his friend looked at each other. Then this famous author, who SHOULD know the power of words, said to me, "Wow! If we would have known you were going to be this pretty, we would have been much nicer to you." There were no words I could come up with. It was a confirmation to me that all the "mean school stuff" really happened. I excused myself and decided (after a couple more really odd interactions) that I needed to go home.

So now we flash forward to the thirty-year reunion. I saw this same famous author standing at the bar. I walked up to him and said, "Do you have a minute? I'd like to sit down and talk to you." His response, "Oh, what shitty thing did I do to you?" My thought was, maybe I wasn't the first one to want to get something off my chest. We sat down and started to talk. I recounted the ten-year reunion conversation we had. I reminded him of the power of words. I also told him I hadn't lost any sleep over it, but I thought it would be a good thing for me to let him know how I felt about it. As he was about to say something, a drunk woman (a mean girl associate) decided to come over and literally drape herself over me and say a big slurred "hi" to me. Mr. Famous Author asked her to give us a minute because we were talking. She made her stumbling exit. So back to what he said; he sort of apologized. He didn't have much recollection of the encounter. For me, it didn't matter what he remembered. As we were talking, he had a hand in his pocket, and a drink in the other hand. He pulled his hand out of his pocket and out fell a tape recorder. It slid across the floor. He became very nervous, almost panic-stricken. He assured me he wasn't taping any of our conversation. In fact, he "assured" me way too much. I was done with what I had to say anyway. So off I went to find my friends I had arrived with.

In grade school I met this cute, funny girl. We became instant friends. She didn't live very far from me. We would ride bikes together, go to each other's houses, even have sleepovers. Even back then my friendships felt deep and important. She and I were seemingly inseparable. We were extremely close in junior high as well. In fact, we were friends all through school and continued our close friendship after we graduated from high school. I loved her so much.

Around the time I started having my anxiety disorder and subsequent agoraphobia, it was tough for me to get out and around, especially by myself. When I was housebound, people would come over to visit. It wasn't an easy time to say the least. My friend had met someone and gotten engaged. She was excitedly planning her wedding. Of course I would shore myself up to be able to go to her wedding! I didn't think anything would or could keep me away. In fact, I had someone take me shopping to buy a dress so I would be ready for the big day. I was happy and excited for her.

About a month before her wedding, she called me. She wanted to know if I could meet her at a restaurant near my apartment. Being agoraphobic, as hard as that was going to be, I agreed to meet her. I got dressed, hyperventilated, and left my apartment to go to my car. It was all I could do to leave my home. Between my home and the restaurant there were railroad tracks. In my agoraphobic state, those tracks terrified me. The "what-ifs" started to creep in. What if I get to the tracks and there's a train? I will be trapped in my car and in traffic! What if I get on the other side of the tracks and there's a train? I won't be able to get home right away. I will be trapped in my car and in traffic! But I sucked it up and got to the restaurant. I sat in the booth waiting for her. I couldn't imagine what she wanted to talk about that she just couldn't come over to my apartment.

She arrived, sort of smiled at me, and sat down. We ordered coffee and right before we ordered anything to eat she said to me, "I don't want you at my wedding. You're far too depressing to be with." I sat there in stunned silence. Then she said, "That's what I wanted to tell you." And then she got up and left. I was devastated. I couldn't cry, I couldn't speak, I couldn't drink my coffee. I finally was able to ask for the check. Oh, she left me to pay for the coffee too. Wow! We didn't speak again until…

After I had been married for a few years, I came home to a voice-mail message on my answering machine. It was that same woman, the one that left me in the restaurant to pay for her coffee. The voice mail was a kind of rambling message, a little hard to understand. What I did get from it was she wanted to meet for lunch, and she wanted to know what would be convenient for me. She was in from out of town for just a few days. Evidently she had moved to Arizona. I called her back, and she was a bit cryptic about why she wanted to meet. I thought it would be appropriate to go back to the same restaurant she left me at years before. Why not? I didn't want to ruin the vibe of a restaurant I really liked if she was going to devastate me all over again. We met the next day. I was in a booth waiting for her. She sort of smiled at me as she sat down. I asked her how her husband was. She told me they had divorced, she had met this other man, and they moved to Arizona together. There was a little small talk. I just couldn't imagine what this was about. But I wasn't going to rush her. She seemed different, slower, more thoughtful. She started by saying she thought she owed me an apology. OK. For what, I thought to myself. Where is this going? She wanted to tell me a terrible story. She started by telling me that in Arizona she was working for this interior design company, at least that is my recollection now. She had been working there for a while. She was very happy with her life. One day at work she had gone into the women's bathroom and into one of the stalls. The door to the stall had somehow detached and fell on her head. She had been injured and diagnosed with a traumatic brain injury. While in the hospital, she started to suffer with a panic disorder and agoraphobia. This injury changed her whole life. Somewhere in all of her suffering, she realized what I had been going through. What she had said about me being "far too depressing to be around" when referring to me years earlier, she now knew what it was like and she owed me an apology for being so uncaring and judgmental. I just stared at her. I told her how sorry I was that had happened to her. Most importantly, I wanted her to know I would never have wished that on her or anyone for that matter. After that, I don't remember anything else from that meeting. It could have been my PTSD that had me tune out for the rest of the time, or maybe other things were just too painful to remember. I know I got home just fine. That was the last time I heard from her, which really is OK by me. I want to say karma is a bitch, but do I really feel that way? Not really. Well…

CHAPTER 8

Education and Vocation

I thought it would be a good idea to include my educational background, as well as my vocational history.

Preschool: Known as nursery school when I was little. I don't remember a lot. It was a Jewish nursery school at a synagogue. I can't recall anything of consequence.

Kindergarten: This was at the local grade school. I loved my teacher. She was sweet. The thing that I remember most is stringing cranberries and popcorn for our classroom Christmas tree. Back then no one made a stink about it. It was fun. Of course I had never done it before, being Jewish and all. But we did hang stockings on the fireplace at home. Hmmmm.

First Grade: My teacher was loving and nurturing. She taught us math by using bundles of Popsicle sticks.

Second Grade: Was rough. My teacher wasn't very warm and nurturing. In fact, she seemed unhappy and cross. I was afraid of her. She was the teacher who got me sent to the office when my mom asked me to talk to the lunch ladies.

Third Grade: I can't come up with anything. Maybe it was uneventful.

Fourth Grade: I liked my teacher a lot but was also leery around her. She laughed at students. Not in the laugh-with-you sense but a belittling laugh-at-you way. I wanted her to like me. She made fun of the way I kept the inside of my desk. She called me "Pig Pen" in front of the other kids. They laughed. I took it to heart. I heard it as I was "Pig Pen." Many years later she was my stepson's fourth-grade teacher. She had married and changed her last name. But I would have recognized her anywhere.

Fifth Grade: The teacher seemed much older than the others. Certainly more old-fashioned. She kicked me out of a spelling bee because she thought I was using sign language to help another student spell a word. I wasn't, but I had to sit down anyway.

Sixth Grade: Was traumatic. The teacher was loud, obnoxious, and cruel. He would make sure to single students out and tell them they were stupid in front of the whole class. He did that to me once, and I started crying uncontrollably. A very brave sixth-grade student stood up and told him to leave me alone (that person is a Rabbi now). This teacher would read poetry and pound his fists on the desks of students. It was all quite frightening. His behavior was so odd. You just never knew what he was going to do next. Would he yell, would he tell a joke, lie to us about textbooks not being available, rant, belittle? Which personality would show up for class each day? I was terrified every day. Again, I was mostly terrified of everything all of the time.

Years later I was told he had died of liver failure. He had a terrible drinking problem for years. Well, that explained everything. Explained, but didn't excuse him for his behavior.

I noticed a big difference between fifth and sixth grade. Kids were meaner, more judgmental, and cruel. I don't know why, but things got so much harder for me. I thought maybe junior high would be different. Oh, how wrong I would be.

Junior High: I participated in a lot of extracurricular activities. I was in choir; I played on the volleyball and basketball teams. I made some friends. But my most important meeting would become part of my long-term core group. She would be my best friend in junior high. We went through the same boy-crazy stage together. She was probably the first friend I had to accept me as I was and continues to accept as I am. More about her later.

Academically I did all right. I was a B student, some Cs. But when it came to math, I had such trouble. I just couldn't grasp geometry. It didn't make sense to me. I just couldn't get more than a D. Way back then not a lot was known about dyslexia. At one point my mom told me she had trouble with math in school. I didn't know what that had to do with me having the problems I was having. My parents hired a math tutor to help me. Even with the tutor, I couldn't grasp geometry. I tried and tried. I didn't want to fail the class because I didn't want to take it over. So the day came when the geometry final was being given. Honestly, it was all so confusing for me. I did my best on the test and waited for the results. A couple of days later I got my grade…D-. How could that be? I studied, I worked hard! But at least I squeaked by and didn't have to repeat the class. I brought home my test with the D- on it and Mom said, "I should have never told you I had trouble in math when I was in school. It just gave you an excuse not to try." Wow! Thank goodness I didn't go into a field where I had to use math as a mainstay of making a living. I have an accountant and a personal banker I consult with regularly. I trust them implicitly.

Anything that was English-based, I could pass with flying colors. I excelled at writing. Reading was tougher. But then again, no one knew very much, if anything, about dyslexia back then.

It seemed to me that "mean girls" came to power during junior high. They were cruel. They were judgmental. They were trouble. Little did I know how much worse they would get. I tried out for the school dance line in ninth grade. I tried out because I loved to dance. I wish I would have known it was about being popular and not being talented. I made it in as an alternate. What that meant was I would have to be at every practice, even though I probably wouldn't dance. I had to know all of the girls' dance steps in case I had to sub for them if someone was sick. There were four or five alternates, one for every unit. Some of the time the alternates went to games even if they weren't subbing for someone. I think my favorite (insert sarcasm) story would be...I was at a college football game where the dance line was dancing. I was watching from the stands. It "appeared" that one of the girls got woozy and had to be taken off the sidelines. I was asked to sub for her. I had no costumes of my own. Alternates were not allowed to buy any. So I had to put this girl's sweaty costume on and sub for her. I can still remember how it felt to put on that wet, sweaty, smelly sequined costume. It sends shivers down my spine thinking about how gross it was. Turns out, she was hungover and didn't feel like dancing anymore. She didn't know that I heard her tell someone that. But that was my job as an alternate. It was what was expected. What I SHOULD do. That wouldn't be the first or last time that would happen. So I figured I'd automatically be made a full-fledged dance line member when tryouts came around. Nope. They made all the alternates try out all over again. My friends tried out with me. None of us made it in. Not even me! I wanted to know why. I called the director of the dance line, and she told me, "After speaking with all of the girls, they thought you acted like you were a full-fledged member instead of an alternate." I was hurt and shocked! I was also told that because I didn't drop all of my outside friends, I wasn't wanted in the group. What kind of person would I have been if I could easily have dropped my real friends?

That's how tenth grade started for me. That was followed up by people from the dance line group, who I thought were my friends, not being allowed to talk to me anymore. So every day I saw these people, every day they dismissed me with their eyes and attitudes. Welcome to high school. Some of these were the "mean girls," and the "mean girls" just got meaner. It was painful. They weren't just "mean girls" to me, but to a lot of people. Before there was a movie called *The Mean Girls,* it was a reality at our high school from 1975 to 1977. After hearing about the movie when it came out in 2004, I realized it was a universal theme.

Academically I was an OK student, same as junior high. I excelled in anything English-based. I didn't do so well in math classes. I took a business class. Loved it, loved the teacher. He was funny, smart, and tolerant of all of us smart-asses but wasn't so patient or tolerant when a friend of mine and I got into a perfume fight in his class. The smell of *Tabu* and *Charlie* didn't mix so well. We were kicked out of class and sent to the office. We were assigned detention for the next couple of days. That meant we had to stay after school and sit in the lunchroom for an hour. Then we would have to take the activity bus home. I was in so much trouble at home when my parents found out what had happened. I was grounded for a week. So no more perfume fights ever again.

By the time I was a junior in high school I was doing some drinking and had discovered pot. My buddy "doobie." Doobie helped me get through anything. Well, let me rephrase. Doobie made me zone out of everything. The abuse at home, bad relationships, friendships I didn't know would mend, and school in general. I smoked pot almost every day before school started and almost every night after dinner. If I was lucky, I would be able to smoke pot during a break at school, so that kept me stoned often. I was lucky to be graded on attendance alone. I would sit like a vegetable, stare out the window, and watch the trees blow in the wind. Or I would read a book, inserted into whatever subject book I was supposed to be studying from. I liked that kind of floaty, blank feeling. My best friend and I would walk to her house, put on bikinis, and lay in the sun. I would intercept the letters the school would send to my parents. But I missed one. Boy did I get in trouble when my parents found out how much school I had skipped out of. I still managed to graduate high school, but I wasn't living at my parents' house when I did. I was living with my boyfriend. That was after my dad almost killed me.

The "mean girls" didn't know about what happened with my dad, but they did know I was living with my boyfriend. That was a special kind of hell when they decided to harass me about it. But I didn't owe them an explanation. So I tried to stay under the radar around them. Not easy when I had to see them every day. The day I turned eighteen, I went to the high school office and signed a piece of paper declaring myself an adult. When I didn't want to be in school, I would write myself a note and bring it to the office. It usually said, "I don't feel like being here today. Sincerely, Roberta." The school couldn't do anything about it. I was eighteen in December, school ended in June. I was considered an adult at eighteen. I'm not sure how I managed to graduate, but I guess I must have done enough work and showed up just enough. My grades in high school were Bs and Cs. I was so glad to be done with high school.

Long before there was Columbine, I would have a recurring daydream about being shot in the hallway at school. The daydream involved getting shot on the way to or from the bathroom or on my way to a class. I would be the only one in the hallway, except the shooter. I would be shot in the upper arm, and the shooter would run out of the school. The daydream would continue with people taking care of me and being nice to me. What an odd way to daydream about getting positive attention or what I believed at that time would be positive attention. Reflecting on it now, it wouldn't have been positive attention. It would have been people feeling sorry for me. Of course, I never ever told anyone about my daydream. Not then for sure. I'm just talking about it now. It makes me shake my head how lost I was as a young girl. How lost I would stay for a long time.

I wanted to go to college after I graduated. I wanted to be an English teacher. But I studied the statistics of how likely it would be that I would find a job teaching English after graduating from college. The numbers weren't good. The numbers said there would be a glut of English teachers and not enough jobs to go around. So I opted out of going to college and kept my job selling shoes. I worked retail for years until my anxiety disorder and agoraphobia made it impossible for me to work. I went to therapy as my new "job." I was on disability for a while. When I started seeing the light at the end of the tunnel, and it wasn't the light from an oncoming train, I started to venture out of my house. I decided I was going to go to cosmetology school to get my manicurist license. There was a school not too far from where I was living. I drove up there and got all the information about courses, tuition, and loans. After thinking about it for a few days, I enrolled. I was terrified. I hadn't really left my apartment for about two years. I pushed myself every day to get there. The anxiety was overwhelming and disorienting. But I finally settled into a routine. I studied hard. I was top in my class. I was so proud. It was time to tell people what I was doing, that I was out of my house and going to school. My friends were thrilled and proud. My parents were confused and didn't understand. But they also took advantage of getting manicures from me for free. What I didn't know was when it came time to take my state board test, I had to drive to another city, across the river. I wasn't ready for that. But I carpooled with three of my classmates and I drove. I thought if I drove, I'd feel more in control. Wouldn't you know, it was snowing like crazy that morning. I was terrified and full of anxiety. But I needed to take the test to get my license. I got there and was panic-stricken. But I was top in my class. I'd pass with no problem. A few days later I got a letter in the mail. I had failed my license test. How? I knew that stuff backward and forward. I had to retake the test and had to wait thirty days. Both of my parents took turns calling me stupid. Told me I hadn't paid attention in class, the usual stuff. I studied and studied. I made another appointment to take the test. I think my dad offered to drive me. So I let him. I got there, took the test and a few days later found out I passed with flying colors. Now all I had to do was find a job. When I did, I developed a large clientele and was happy as a manicurist for twenty years.

When my marriage was deteriorating and my mom got sick, I was having trouble working. My anxiety level was so high it was tough for me to leave my house. After my mom died and my marriage was over, I didn't know if I was on foot or on horseback. I'm not exactly sure how it happened, but I accidentally started a business. I was making cold calls for different companies, trying to get their foot in the door of other businesses. That blossomed into Necessity Enterprises, LLC. I now have several clients that I make cold calls for, as well as act as their client services director. I am very proud of my niche business. I work from home and love it! It's a choice to work from home now, not because I am agoraphobic. I like the relationships I have formed with my clients. We all have the same work ethic and work goals. I am proud to say I'm a successful entrepreneur.

CHAPTER 9

Boys to Men
The Relationships

My first real date happened when I was fifteen. I had gone to a New Year's party with a friend and was introduced to him. He was so cute. He asked me if I would go out with him to a movie the following week. I told him I had to talk to my parents about it. Whenever the topic of dating came up at home, my folks said I couldn't date until I was sixteen. I don't know why, but when I asked them, they said it would be OK. So the following week, he and I double-dated with our friends. I was dressed in nice dark green corduroy pants and a soft, green argyle patterned sweater. Brand new, of course. I was wearing a mid-length navy blue wool coat. Good thing I had that coat on because we stood in line outside for quite some time to see *The Exorcist*. I had read the book; how much scarier could the movie be? Oh, my naiveté. I was so terrified during the movie I think I watched most of it through my fingers while I covered my face. I had never seen anything like that before. I was so scared I felt sick. But I didn't want to be a baby, so I sat through the whole thing. The guys thought the movie was funny and fakey, or so they said. I don't remember my girlfriend saying much of anything. I can tell you that I didn't sleep well for months. After the movie we all went to see the "submarine races." Yeah, what did I know? I didn't see any submarines, but I did get to make out with my date.

Around this time I had contracted mono. I was getting sicker and sicker, but the mono tests kept coming back negative. Of course I thought I was probably possessed. Mono is known as "the kissing disease." It's also thought when you have mono you sleep a lot. But when you have severe mono coupled with hepatitis, you can't sleep because you become paranoid. Good timing for me, right? Why wouldn't I think I was possessed?! In fact, the doctor told me it was one of the most severe cases of mono they had ever seen.

By this time my parents had gone on vacation and left my sister and her first husband to take care of me. The doctor called my parents and told them how sick I was. He suggested they fly me out to California where they were vacationing so that I could rest. Obviously the doctor didn't know anything about what went on with my family. I ended up missing a total of three months of school. Before I flew to California, my neighbor would pick up my homework from my teachers. When I finished, he would bring the completed work back to my teachers. It's a wonder I graduated from junior high.

I met my first serious boyfriend when I was a sophomore in high school. We would do all the things high school kids did. We'd go to concerts, out to dinner, movies. What I hadn't done with other boys was have sex. I had kissed a couple of boys, but that was pretty much the extent of it. It seemed to me a lot of girls I knew were already having sex. So as my boyfriend and I spent more time together, the subject started to arise (yes, that pun is intended). I think we had been dating about six months. I had no idea what sex entailed. But it was "all the buzz" around school. After some discussion, my boyfriend convinced me that once we "did it" I would want to rip his clothes off all of the time. It would be fun! One night we were at his parents' house. They were upstairs; we were downstairs in the den. We were making out and things got moving really fast. This was the night I was going to lose my virginity. He tried and tried to get inside me. It wasn't working like I thought it was supposed to, and more importantly, it hurt! I was starting to groan (as opposed to moan) and told him it hurt. He assured me we were "almost there." I felt myself chickening out. It hurt too much. I told him how much it hurt. The next thing I knew, he put a pillow over my face and forced himself inside me. It was excruciating! I was crying. He held me and when he was done he told me it would get easier. All I kept thinking was, is this what everyone is talking about? I didn't realize what truly had just happened. I thought the first time for everyone was like that. Remember, I was scared of everything all of the time. But I knew I had made him happy. Wasn't that why we were together? Isn't that what I SHOULD have done? We continued to have sex. I continued to read up on different techniques. I asked him one day why he didn't go down on me? I had certainly done that for him. He answered me totally straight-faced, "Eww, that's just gross." It was never talked about again. Several months later I skipped a period. I was scared, and I SHOULD have been. In 1976, I was pregnant in high school. What was I going to do? I talked to my boyfriend about it, and he thought I must have been mistaken. He took me to a clinic for a pregnancy test. I was not mistaken. I should add here that I have found my journals from 1975 to 1976 so all of this was documented. I was taking Forkner Shorthand in school and everything I wanted to hide from my parents I wrote in shorthand. Forty years after writing it, I can still read it. So now we had to face some kind of decision. According to my journal and my memory, he said, "I can always deny it's mine because you've got a reputation." Wow! How could I have a reputation if he was the only person I had been with?

A week or so after learning I was pregnant, a bunch of us went on a ski trip. I had terrible morning sickness (all day). Skiing was not my top priority. Making a decision and keeping that decision from my parents was critical. Regardless of the circumstance, on that ski trip my boyfriend woke me up at 4:00 a.m. to have sex, where I promptly quoted Elton John, "It's four in the morning dammit, listen to me good." We decided I would have an abortion. Luckily (for lack of a better word) that was the first year a girl of sixteen or seventeen didn't need parental consent. If my parents would have found out, they would have sent me away for sure. What was required by law was four hours of counseling: individual, group, birth-control choices, and what to do for follow-up appointments. The woman who was in charge of that four hours was a lovely, warm person. She offered to be in the room with any of us (I think there were four other girls). My girlfriend came with me when my boyfriend dropped me off at the clinic. Yes, I said, "dropped me off." He had to take his mom to the beauty shop. So there I was with my girlfriend, waiting to be taken in to an exam room for "the procedure." My girlfriend stayed in the waiting room when the nurse took me back. I lay there while they examined me. I was scared and numb all at the same time. As I was waiting for the doctor to come in, a counselor entered the room. I thought good, someone I could talk to. She came around the table, looked me in the eye, and said, "You know you're being punished, don't you?" She went on quoting bible verses. Then she slipped out the door. What just happened? Was this part of the four hours of counseling? It was awful! It seemed inappropriate, especially at such a vulnerable time. The doctor came in and did the procedure. He was nice, calming, caring. He told me what to expect as far as bleeding. He told me I would be given antibiotics, and I couldn't have sex for six weeks. That was the last thing on my mind. My mind was reeling. I spent the night at my girlfriend's house. She looked after me. I was so lucky I could escape there. That was a secret kept until my late twenties. How does that go? You're only as sick as your secrets? Boy, did I have a lot of them. I didn't even realize how many until much later.

Flash forward probably eight years. I ran into the warm, lovely counselor from the clinic. We were standing in line at a restaurant. I told her she looked familiar and then I realized who she was. I told her that her demeanor was what got me through that terrible, tough day at the clinic. Then I mentioned the Bible-quoting, Jesus-talking woman. She said to me, "Oh, my G-d, we were looking for her. We heard someone was doing that, we just didn't know who. Why didn't you say something?" I told her I figured it was part of the four-hour counseling thing. She apologized to me for being subjected to that and assured me that was not part of the program. Of course that woman found me. She could see how guilt-ridden and scared I was.

A few months ago I had coffee with my first serious boyfriend, the man who took my virginity. He is now an attorney. I wanted to let him know I was writing a book about my life. I assured him I wasn't using any names. Attorneys make me nervous. They're so... so...litigious!

I did my share of dating in high school. I had a couple of boyfriends I slept with. It seemed like the thing to do. It also seemed empowering for me. I didn't really understand why. It was a fun thing to do and made me happy, for lack of a better term.

Another high school romance was what I would call a trophy romance. He was handsome, popular, funny, and drove a nice car. I also thought he could be "the one." What did I know? I was seventeen. We had a lot of fun together. We went to lots of high school parties where I did my fair share of underage drinking. One of the most memorable nights, we were at this party and I started drinking Everclear (100% vodka) topped off with a little lemonade just to make the liquor go down easier. I don't know where my boyfriend was while I was getting totally smashed, but I know someone went to get him when I fell into the kitchen sink. I had been sitting on the kitchen counter, got drunk, and fell into the sink. He came in to the kitchen and told me it was probably time to leave. I walked outside with him and lay down on the grass. I wouldn't get up until he promised I could drive his car. I know! We were so young and so foolish. Both of us, because he let me drive myself home. He helped me out of the car, got me inside (thankfully my parents were out for the evening) and got me into my room. The next thing I knew, it was the middle of the night, and I was still in my clothes from the party. I got up, put on pajamas, brushed my teeth, realized I was still drunk, got into bed, and fell asleep. I woke up around 8:00 a.m. It was Sunday and I had to go to the synagogue where I was an assistant teacher. Problem...I was still a little tipsy. There was no way I could call in sick without alerting my parents that I had been drinking. So off I went to teach. I also had a job at a retail clothing store that I had to be at. It was a very long day.

Getting back to the boyfriend part of this, I really liked him. I don't remember how long we were together, I think only a few months. But in that time we had started sleeping together. He was fun, kind of shy about having sex, and I wasn't very experienced. I didn't know why he would be shy. Isn't sex what guys wanted?

We loved to get dressed in that seventies fashion. We looked good together. He and I went to a prom-like dance together. We coordinated our outfits, my apricot dress with the peach-colored ties and his peach-colored tux. Ah, the seventies. It was quite a night. We started off at dinner, went to the dance, then to his grandmother's empty house. We had great sex and then had to get me back home before my curfew. On the way home I realized I forgot my gold hoop earrings on the nightstand at his grandma's house. He dropped me at home, kissed me good night, and then went back to retrieve my earrings, which he gave me the next time we got together. Our high school romance started fast and ended pretty quickly. He broke up with me, telling me it was all "too much" for him. I returned the tiger eye ring and bracelet he had given me and was heartbroken. There was a lot of "hormonal" drama in high school.

I don't know how different I was than any other high school girl. Every relationship, at least in my mind, was going to be "the one." I don't know where that comes from. The breakups were so heart-wrenching. By the way, he and I run into each other period-ically now. We're always cordial. Years after we broke up someone told me I was his first. That would be difficult for me to believe, but maybe that was where the shyness came from. Just a few years ago I was told that this guy's dad watched us having sex through a hole in the paneling at his house. Holy crap! I don't know how to even verify either one of those stories.

My next boyfriend was my best friend's boyfriend's best friend. Did you get that? Doesn't matter. It started out as casual double dat-ing. We had a lot of fun together. When I met this guy, he had just broken his leg in gymnastic practice. So if he picked me up for a date, he would drive left-footed and have his right leg up on the bench seat behind me. Good thing he was a gymnast…flexibility! I really liked him. He was funny, smart, and kind of brash. His parents really liked me. My parents, hard to tell if they liked him, or anyone I dated for that matter. But they were nice to him. I know I've said that each relationship was "the one." But I really thought he was "the one" for sure. We got along really well, except for an argument we had in Civics class. We were on opposite sides of the issue, and it got heated. It carried over into our relationship. In fact, I wrote a not-so-flattering story about him in my Moffett class. But we worked things out. Just a funny side note, he and I are still friends, and one day we were talking about this Civics class incident. I referenced myself as his girlfriend back then. We had dated for about a year and a half. He told me he never thought of me as his girlfriend. Isn't that interesting? Kind of funny. I always thought he was my boyfriend for that year and a half. Go figure. But I digress. In all the time we went out, we only slept together once. We got really high, and he put on the long disco version of Donna Summer's "Love to Love You Baby" on the record player. Now why would I think I was his girlfriend? That summer he went away to work at a camp. Our high school romance was done.

After my dad had nearly beaten me to death and I ran away, I ended up at my new boyfriend's college dorm. We then moved out of his dorm and found an apartment where we would become caretakers. Not my choice of a job, but where else was I going to go? My impression was this guy was going to take care of me. He was completely horrified by the beating I took from my dad. All I knew was I couldn't live with my parents, not with as terrified as I was of my father. I continued to go to high school, and I wanted to graduate. So caretaker by night, high schooler by day. There was a lot of talk at school about me living with my boyfriend. But I never discussed it with anyone except my best friend. The day of my graduation this guy and I got into an argument. I don't remember what it was about, but I can tell you we were in his car. We were driving down the highway yelling at each other. He pulled over to the shoulder, stopped the car, and told me to get out. So I got out. He drove away leaving me on the highway. I had to get back to the apartment to get my cap and gown. So I started walking. From then on it's blank until the actual graduation ceremony. I stood with the rest of the class before we were ushered to our chairs. People were passing joints and laughing.

I did walk up and collect my diploma. Through all of the trials and tribulations, I graduated!

That night was our senior party. It was an overnight party at the junior high building. The rules were, you had to stay all night. If you left before morning, you couldn't come back in. Disco was just getting started in 1977. The school hired some terrible band that played 1960s psychedelic-type music. The party was kind of a bore, but my friend and I stayed all night. When I got home to the apartment, my boyfriend was angry. He wanted to know where I had been. He knew I was at my senior party. He was yelling at me about cheating on him. He was accusing me of being with some guy all night. The only other thing I remember from that day was one of our birds died that night. I think Elvis Presley died that night too. At least that's how it's connected in my mind.

Things calmed down. He realized I was telling the truth. Life went on. We continued to live together. I cleaned apartments and hallways. I made a home for us. He worked where? I don't even remember. One night we had invited some friends over for drinks before we were all going to go out. Our friends arrived, and we sat around talking and laughing. My boyfriend got up to pour a drink. I asked him to pour me a Coke. I held my glass out, he poured the Coke, and he grabbed my arm and started pulling me toward the counter. He was starting to hurt me, and I quietly asked him to let me go. He pulled harder until my ribs were digging into the corner of the counter. I didn't want to create a scene in front of our friends. I asked him again and told him he was hurting me. He wasn't listening. So I shook my glass of Coke at him so it splashed a little. He became enraged! He wound up and hit me in the head with the glass Coke bottle and poured the rest of what was in the bottle over my head. The next thing I remember was being in the bathroom with the woman friend of mine, washing Coke out of my hair. I don't remember anything else, not from that night and not for the rest of that relationship. I do remember thinking at the precise minute he hit me in the head with the bottle, "What is more humiliating, getting beaten up by my boyfriend or being beaten up by my father?" Obviously neither would be a good choice for me.

Years later I ran into the woman who was in the bathroom with me that night. She had to reintroduce herself to me. I didn't remember her. She wanted to ask me something about that night. She wanted to know how I pulled myself together and went out that night. I was stunned. I said, "We went out?" She told me that not only did we go to dinner, but we went to a movie too. I told her I had no recollection past she and I in the bathroom together. I couldn't even tell her when or how the relationship ended. If I'm not mistaken, I moved back to my parents after he and I broke up.

My next relationship was truly the one that got away, my own fault, really. I met him at the apartment complex I was living at. He was the maintenance guy when I was the caretaker. We had become friends. We didn't start dating until several months after my breakup. He was sweet, kind, funny, self-sufficient, easy to talk to, and easy to be with. He was like the Patrick Swayze character in *Dirty Dancing*, sweet and sensitive, with a wild—but not too wild—side. He drove a 1956 Belvedere. He loved that car. He had a motorcycle too. He wasn't like anyone else I had ever dated. Best thing, he liked me for me. We fell madly in love. Of course, my parents disapproved. At one point my mother threw herself up against the front door and wouldn't let me go outside where he was waiting for me. She said I couldn't go out with him because he was "no more than a janitor." (Ironically, he became a school janitor in another state when he moved away and married his high school sweetheart). I didn't understand what that meant for her. For me, it meant he had a job he liked, a life he liked and was a responsible adult. After I peeled her off the door, I joined him in his '56 Belvedere and off we went to dinner and a movie. He and I moved in together several months later.

It was a great, healthy relationship. We were so happy. We lived together for quite a while and started talking about getting married. He wasn't sold on the idea but said he would think about it. We became engaged about three months later. I don't know what happened to me. I started thinking maybe this wasn't a good idea. He was great! He took care of me when I was sick and vice versa. He was creative, he was an artist, he was responsible. He was gorgeous and best of all, he wasn't violent. I became uneasy, distracted, then…I cheated on him. How could I have done something so awful? I'm not a cheater. What was I thinking? I tried to keep it together, but no such luck. Inevitably we split after three years of being together. I couldn't figure out what was wrong with me. Well, duh, 20-20 hindsight, I sabotaged the only good relationship I had known and may ever know. I may not have been stupid, careless, or lazy but I obviously felt undeserving of happiness. I can honestly say he was the love of my lifetime. Last I heard he was still married to his high school sweetheart and is retired from being a janitor. I also heard he was painting. Good for him. I wish him nothing but happiness.

After that my life went haywire. Poor choices…in men especially. I fell into a fast crowd. I'm lucky I lived to tell the tale.

For my twenty-second birthday my friends and I went out to a male strip club. Now that was an experience. I had never been to any kind of strip show before. The first dancer that came out looked like my last boyfriend. All my friends yelled out his name. It was uncanny how much they looked alike. Being at this strip club with lots of one-dollar bills was really exciting. There was such a naughty but cool energy in the place. The dancer who looked like my ex-boyfriend danced right up to me. I tucked the first dollar bill into his G-string. It was thrilling. My girlfriends were having fun too. More dancers came out on the stage; honestly, it was like being in a candy store. It definitely was a low-budget Chippendales but not trashy. My girlfriends and I were there for two to three hours. Happy birthday to me! We decided we had enough and got up to leave. As we were going out the door, the first dancer ran up to me and asked if he could see me again. He asked for my phone number and gave me his. Sure, why not? That would be the beginning of trouble for me. It was the eighties. The decade that I dubbed, "I'll take one of those to go with nothing on it." Now it's called "hooking up." It was a time for freewheeling sex, nothing more, nothing less. This guy was just the first in a series of male stripper hookups for me. It became addicting to go to the shows to hang out with these guys and then sleep with them. There were several I hooked up with. There were a couple that were very dangerous and bad news. But as I said, it was addicting: the energy, the amazing sex, and the unpredictability. The most dangerous, and of course the one I fell in love with was, well, let's just call him "D" for Dangerous. D was intense, he was handsome, he was funny at times. He had tattoos and a barrel chest. He fascinated me. He was really good at getting me to do just about anything. I'd drive him to his strip shows or private parties and pick him up afterward. At one point he moved in with me. He really didn't have much stuff—a gym bag full of clothes and a shaving kit. He smoked pot; sometimes I would smoke with him. He took different kinds of pills like quaaludes, brown and clears, tranquilizers, none of which I was interested in trying. He was really into shooting up crystal meth and sometimes heroin or coke. He was drug addicted. This was a real compromise to how I lived. He would shoplift to support his habit. He'd even have me come along. This was not how I lived my life. But I "loved" him.

One day he wanted to borrow my car, and I let him. He didn't come back for what I think was two days. I had to go out searching. I had a good idea where he might be. And there was my car, in front of his ex-girlfriend's house. I had my extra set of keys and took my car back. He got a ride over to my house and apologized, asked me to forgive him. He said it wouldn't happen again. Then everything changed. He became horribly violent. The first time he beat me up I ended up in the emergency room. I heard myself say, "I fell down the stairs." He came over and of course he apologized and begged me to take him back. He explained how it had happened, and he would make sure it would never happen again. You know all those Lifetime movies where you can't believe that a woman takes a man back after he beats her? D and I were on and off for four years. But not how you would think. The very last time he beat me up, he nearly broke my arm while whipping me into a wall. Something tore under my shoulder blade. In fact, it is an injury that flares up to this day, as well as others he inflicted. He managed to give me herpes in the time that we were together. There is nothing like not being able to forget an old relationship. But I consider myself lucky that's all I contracted from him, especially being he was an intravenous drug user.

I finally filed a restraining order against him. He would break the order by showing up at my work or breaking into my apartment.

I think I filed a total of four restraining orders. The problem with the restraining orders back then was the order would list the address of where I was. So there he'd be. The last year or two of our four-year relationship was about filing restraining orders and going to court. The last year he was stalking me. It was during this time that I considered killing myself. I wanted to end all of the pain of what was going on. Again, thank goodness for the Animal Humane Society.

After meeting all of these strippers, I adopted their sexually carefree attitude. To go even further, I would admit to being borderline sexually addicted. It was the freest I ever felt about myself. I could have fun, I could role play, I could experiment. The other part of meeting them was dealing with true bad boys. There were drugs, there was theft, and there were guns.

I got a call in the middle of the night from one of these guys. He was in a panic. He thought he had overdosed on cocaine and was terrified he was going to die. Being the "fixer" that I am, I told him I would call him an ambulance and meet him at the hospital. He became even more agitated and paranoid. He wanted me to come over and take care of him. So I got dressed and drove as fast as I could to get there. I got up to his door, knocked, and heard the doorknob turn. This guy opened the door, pointing a loaded gun at my head. I don't know where it came from, but I stayed calm, said his name several times, and reminded him who I was and that he had called me to come help him. We stood there for I don't know how long and he finally lowered his gun. He asked me to come in. And there I stayed for the next several hours until he came down off his high. A gun in my face had never happened to me before, nor has it happened since. Who were these people and why was I involved? Their addiction was drugs, mine was codependence or addiction to excitement and the unpredictability of various situations.

At the end of the court stuff and that relationship, I met my next boyfriend. It was Memorial Day in 1985. He was someone I dated in high school. He had his two little boys with him. He was going through a divorce. He asked for my number. The next day he called and wanted to know if he could get a manicure from me. I had the time open at the salon. He showed up. We talked while I gave him his manicure. He went up to pay at the register, and he realized he forgot his wallet. I laughed at him and teased him about trying to get a freebie. I told him not to worry about it. Later that day a huge bouquet of roses arrived with a card apologizing and asking me out for the following week. How romantic! I said yes. We had dated for a few weeks when he agreed to come to my last court date regarding my ex-boyfriend. It was nice to have him there dressed in a suit, looking like an attorney. I felt protected. Even though I was still having terrible nightmares about D, I was ready to move forward in my life.

I was renting the basement of a house when we started dating. It was not ideal, but it did keep me out of the elements. About a month after we started dating, he was supposed to spend the night but he didn't show up. I couldn't imagine where he was. He called the next day as if nothing was wrong. I reminded him he said he was going to spend the night. I told him I had even powdered the sheets with his favorite perfume of mine...Raffinee. With an, "Oh, my G-d, I'm sorry, but the guys and I were playing poker and I spaced it out. Will you forgive me?" He promised to make it up to me. I forgave him.

We dated about six months before we started house hunting. I was spending nights at his apartment if his kids weren't there. We spent a lot of time together. It seemed like the logical next step. Our house hunting went on for about a month. Then we found the cutest three-bedroom rambler across the street from a small lake. We later found out it was called "A lake with a ponding area." We put a bid in on it, and with some negotiating we got it! He called me at work to let me know. We went to dinner to celebrate. He was telling me about the negotiations. He was very proud to admit that, "If they don't call you an asshole when the negotiating was done, then you left money on the table." I thought he was kidding and didn't think much of it. I now know those are the things you pay attention to.

About a month later we moved into our home. We had some new carpeting put in, had some redecorating and cleaning to do. But it really felt like ours. We had done it up in art-deco style. Pretty severe, but tasteful, black lacquer furniture, rose-colored carpeting, black couch and chair in the living room. The den was more kid friendly, vinyl couch, easy to clean. That was the family room. The kids were really young. We had twin beds in one room for them. They were with us three to four days a week. There were also two dogs that came into our custody from his ex-wife. I remember the first night that the kids and the dogs were there. We all said good night and got into bed. My boyfriend (not yet my husband) was in the kids' room telling them a story. I was happy, nervous, but happy. The kids were finally asleep. My boyfriend came to bed. All was right with the world. Until…I heard this squeaking noise. I got up to check it out. The youngest boy was grinding his teeth. The older boy was talking in his sleep. I got back into bed. As long as I knew what the sounds were, I would be OK. Then my boyfriend began to snore really loudly. I just lay there. You'd think nothing else could happen, right? Wrong. The schnauzer who was lying on the bed with us and the other dog who was under the covers on my side of the bed both started to snore. My eyes were as big as saucers! I thought to myself, what did I get myself into?

There were some bumps along the way, but we were happy together. I loved his kids, I loved his parents, and I was sure I loved him enough to make it work. I knew I didn't want to "date" anymore. HIV/AIDS was now a daily news topic. My mother had been diagnosed with cancer, and I wanted her to be able to join my father in walking me down the aisle if the opportunity ever presented itself.

I had the day off from work; he was out making sales calls. We didn't have the kids that night. What a perfect time for romance and seduction! As soon as he went out the door, I started planning the surprise evening. I spent the beginning of the day shopping for some sexy lingerie. Bought it, brought it home, and washed it. The next several hours I cooked all the things I thought he'd like. I made sure to have his favorite cocktail on hand. I cut everything up into bite-sized pieces. I realized he was going to be home in an hour, so I took a shower and got into the sexy lingerie. What I didn't have time to do was clean up the pots and pans in the sink. So I closed off the kitchen with the pocket doors. I ran downstairs and put *9 ½ Weeks* in the VCR (it was 1986, yes, VCR) and ran back upstairs. I placed a blindfold on the table and waited for him to come home. He walked in and saw the dining room table set beautifully, scarves and a blindfold on his chair. He looked at me and said, "What's this?" I told him…dinner. So he changed into something more comfortable and sat down at the table. I proceeded to tie his hands behind his back and put the blindfold on him. I promised there were no tricks or pranks, just dinner. I had all kinds of dipping sauces and meats, as well as his cocktail. It was all very sexy! When he said he was done eating, I led him downstairs and popped in the movie. Again, very sexy until…he took a pair of scissors and cut my brand new lingerie off of me. But, I wasn't going to let that ruin the evening. I went with it. We made love and watched the movie. It was quite an evening, if I do say so myself. When the movie was over, we walked upstairs. He opened the pocket doors and saw the kitchen. He started yelling at me about how messy the kitchen was. How could I leave pots and pans in the sink? Why didn't I clean this up before he got home? I stood there agog. I couldn't even speak. He decided to go to bed. I cleaned up the kitchen. My head was swimming. I just kept asking myself, how could he be so insensitive and unappreciative? I couldn't believe it. I stayed up and thought carefully about what I wanted to do next.

He woke up at his usual time to get ready for work. I didn't have much to say. He left for work. I called my mom and asked her if I could move back in until I found a place of my own. I packed all of my clothes, shoes, makeup, and anything that belonged just to me, and loaded my car and drove to my parents' house. Not exactly the game plan I had in mind, but it was only temporary.

He came home from work to find me and my stuff gone. I think I left a note for him explaining how hurt I was and how unap-preciated I felt, that I had to think it through regarding our relation-ship. He drove over to my parents' house and we sat outside talking. I was crying. I really had been devastated. Of course he apologized. He wanted me to come back home. I told him I needed time to think. It took me a few days and lots of talking, but I moved back to our house. He promised nothing like that would ever happen again. I believed him. *Oy!*

We went back to getting along. He made an effort to be more sensitive. We settled into being together, being in love with each other. We coparented nicely with his ex-wife and ex-in laws. We were quite a mature blended extended family. I liked it. Several months went by and no real complaints. I was getting ready to leave to go to the gym, and he called me into the den. He was lying down on the couch. He asked me to sit on his lap. The only real way to do that was to straddle his legs. I sat on top of him, he looked me in the eye and said, "Let's do it." I reminded him I was going to the gym, and we could "do it" when I got home. "No," he said, let's do it." Again, I repeated myself. He said, "No, let's get married." What? The worst proposal ever! I told him we could talk more about it when I got back. I really didn't know if I SHOULD take him seriously. "Let's do it" as a proposal? Let's not until you find a better way to propose, was what I really wanted to say. I went to the gym. When I got home, he brought me downstairs where his whole jewelry line was laid out on the bar. He told me to pick my ring (all samples, all CZs). I should probably mention he was in the jewelry and diamond business. And that, my friends, was my romantic (not) proposal and ring presentation. I married him anyway. I thought I loved him enough. I definitely loved his mom and dad and his kids. How bad could it get? How long do you have?

The wedding planning started, and he told me he didn't want to have anything to do with it. He just wanted to show up. He was going to pick out his own suit and that was it. Everything else was up to me, including his kids' tux rental and shoes. I decided on tux rental because they were little and growing. Why buy something that wouldn't fit a month from then? The only thing I insisted on was black tennis shoes, something comfortable that they could wear until they grew out of them.

Remember how the planning went with my mom? I had six weeks to pull it all together. I got the band, someone I had known for years. I ordered the flowers, got the reception venue. Except for the problems my mother created and making sure the color palette—remember, any shade of rose was adhered to—it came together nicely. My fiancé had a subdued bachelor party given by his brother. I had girls' night out for dinner. I made sure no male strippers were on anyone's agenda. I had since eschewed that behavior. Our prenuptial dinner was beautiful. I was very emotional. Relatives flew in from all over the country. It was lovely. The wedding was the next day. My parents stayed at the hotel with my relatives who flew in, leaving me to be able to stay at their house with my maid of honor and away from my husband-to-be. In retrospect, that seems silly because the limo picked us up at our house, and we rode together to the synagogue. Oh well. I got in the limo and said I had forgotten something. I ran back in our house and put up a "Just Married" sign on the wall behind our bed. Then it was off to have pictures taken.

We arrived, and the bridesmaids and I were in one room, the guys in another. I had my Janet Jackson cassette playing so we could dance around. We all got ready to meet with the photographer. He was a friend of mine for years, and I trusted whatever he wanted to do. He wanted to get a picture of me pinning a flower on my beloved's lapel. I took the flower out of the box; my beloved snatched it out of my hand, pulled the "greens" off the back of the flower, and said, "I told you, I just wanted a flower, no greens." That was news to me. But we got the picture and continued posing, etcetera. His usher friend thought it was fun and funny to unzip my wedding dress while we were standing side-by-side in a group photo. I made the best of the antics. The time had come; we were to line up to walk down the aisle. First my sister and his brother, then my maid of honor and his best man, then the boys in their rented tuxes and black tennis shoes. Then it was my turn. My mother was on one side of me, my father on the other. Just as the harpist started playing "Always," by Atlantic Starr, the photographer ran up the aisle straight at me. He pushed me by my chest with his hand and said, "My camera just broke. Wait here. I have another one in my car." And there I stood with people wondering why I wasn't moving. I heard the door open and there was the photographer motioning me forward. It really wasn't more than a few minutes. But it was interesting. After the ceremony, my sister told me she thought I'd run out the back door. Kind of funny, but not really my MO.

We stood under the chuppah (Jewish bridal canopy) as our Rabbi talked to us. My uncle, also a Rabbi, took part in marrying us too. It was lovely. It felt warm and welcoming. I looked over and my youngest almost stepchild (he was four and a half) was bouncing his back on one of the poles of the chuppah. As the chuppah swayed gently, I tried to get his attention so he would stop. I was afraid the chuppah would detach and collapse. When I finally got his attention, I whispered, "Don't bounce." He whispered, "What?" I said, "Do you want to sit with your grandma?" He said, "What?" I said it again and loudly he said, "WHAT?" I told him to go sit with his grandma, which he did.

It came time to drink the wine and break the glass. L'Chaim. My almost-husband and I had talked about it. I really didn't want wine; I wasn't much of a drinker. I asked for grape juice, preferably white grape juice in case it spilled. The Rabbi handed the glass to me. I saw it was purple. I told myself to be careful as to not spill on my wedding dress. It was wine, and I nearly choked. My betrothed thought that was funny, me, not so much. We were married despite some glitches. We went onward to our reception. It was beautiful. The food was fabulous, and the band was great! We danced and schmoozed until the wee hours.

The following day we left for our honeymoon up in northern Minnesota. We were gone three days. We were supposed to be gone four days, but there was a huge severe thunderstorm in the city where we lived. The kids called, and they were scared. We watched the news and saw there was flooding where our house was. We packed up our stuff and left the next morning. We got home, and our house was flooded. We had to kick the water-swollen front door to get it open. The basement was flooded, and many items were floating: record albums, clothes, and blankets. What a mess! I started picking stuff up, and he went out to go find a wet-vac. We spent the night and next day cleaning up the basement. I did have to take a break and sleep for a few hours. I never heard the end of how I left him by himself to do "all the work." I wasn't going to argue about it. He could believe whatever he wanted.

We had been married a couple of weeks. Mind you, we had been living together for about a year and half before we got married. I don't know what happens to some people once they get married. A settling in, a freedom to act any way they want, say hurtful things.

I don't know. I will admit in retrospect that he and I may have been twenty-six and twenty-seven, but I don't think either one of us knew what actual marriage entailed. He, being married before, told me it was going to be different for him this time. But I don't believe we had the maturity or understanding of how to make a relationship work.

I just want to lay the framework for what I found shocking and hurtful. We had been married just a couple of weeks. We had gotten into bed and started to make love. At least that's what I thought we were doing. In the middle of the act, he says to me, "You're my whore, my own personal whore." He had never said anything like that to me before. I started to cry and said, "I'm not your whore, I'm your wife." I cried and cried. I couldn't figure out where that came from. Why he thought he had the right to say something so awful and demeaning to me. From that night forward, I found him repulsive. But I was his wife, and I SHOULD have sex with him, right? It was all I could do to feign interest. But I performed my wifely duty, until I couldn't stomach it anymore. The days/nights that he would want to have sex and I said no, he would put a red "X" on the calendar that hung in the kitchen. After a couple of weeks of the "Xs," the kids asked him what the Xs were for. He answered, "Ask Roberta." I don't remember what I said to them when they asked, or even if I addressed it at all. I just knew we weren't going to be OK. That first year was difficult, but we kept it together, sort of.

About three years into the marriage, he was traveling for business a lot. He would come home, and we would have sex. Lather, rinse, repeat. I started not feeling well. I had what seemed to be some sort of odd, severe yeast infection. It just wouldn't go away. I finally went to the doctor and was diagnosed with gardnerella, a sexually transmitted disease. I wasn't having sex with anyone else; hell, I was hardly having sex with my husband. I suddenly remembered a conversation we had while dating. He said hookers didn't count as cheating. I went blank. I never mentioned it to anyone.

Five and a half years went by, and I realized I had had enough of the dysfunction. What kept me hanging in there was my love for his kids and my love for his parents. But was it enough? The kids had already been through one divorce; how would they handle another?

I moved out to an apartment and was only gone about a month. We kept trying to reconcile. I was at the house one day and got a call that his mother had died. He was in the shower when the call came in. I told him as gently as I could. His parents had been living in Florida. I told him to call his dad. I started making calls to friends and family and moved back in. I think that was September 1993. I decided I SHOULD stand by him during this difficult time. I would have to put everything aside. We stuck together and stayed together. In October 1993, his aunt died. In January 1994, our dog died. In March 1994, my mother died. She had myodysplasia that had turned into leukemia.

Let me just back up a bit. A few days before my mother died, and it was apparent it would be soon, my husband became demanding of my time and attention. I spent all day at her house and would come home, and he wouldn't let me sleep. He would turn the bedroom lights on, and if I fell asleep, he would take his key ring and drop it by my head on the headboard. He told me I SHOULD be up and helping him get ready for his jewelry show. He wanted me tagging merchandise. It was all so cruel and surreal, all the while making a good front that our marriage was fine.

As I said, my mother died in March 1994. I got the call at eight in the morning. He, the kids, and I drove over to my parents' house. The odd thing was, he wasn't taking care of me and my feelings the way I took care of him when his mother died. I thought at least I could count on that. He was acting so strangely. That whole day felt like I was slogging through mud and looking at everything through a gelled lens. The hearse pulled up in the driveway. I went outside to look at the interior of it. Why? I don't know.

I think the funeral was two days later. Nothing felt real. We sat with the Rabbi and told stories so he could write the eulogy. The night before the funeral, I asked my husband if the kids could ride with his dad. I knew I needed a quiet ride without any questions. It was the one thing I asked for. He called his dad, and his dad said of course. The next morning the kids were picked up while I was still getting ready. After they went out the door, my husband started needling me about how his kids weren't good enough to ride with me. What a terrible person I was to ask them to go separately. I was emotionally shut down. He continued yelling at me all the way to the synagogue. He pulled up at the door and told me to get out while he parked the car. Really? He was going to let me walk in by myself? In all my numbness, I put one foot in front of the other and walked through the door where I promptly got light-headed and collapsed. Luckily a couple of people caught me before I hit the ground and brought me into the "family room." The next thing I remember was sitting next to my dad in the front pew as he held his "Battle of Midway" hat. He said he brought it with because if he could survive the sinking of the Yorktown in World War II, he could survive this.

After the service my cousin and her husband asked if they could ride with us to the cemetery. They had taken a taxi from the airport and had no car. I was dazed. I must've said yes. All the way to the cemetery my husband kept saying, "Your cousins are good enough to ride with us, but my kids aren't?" I was numb. I do remember seeing the look in my cousin's eyes. But I kept quiet, so did she and her husband.

We got to the cemetery for the graveside service. This is by tradition where relatives can throw dirt on the casket. It's thought of as an honor. To me it was a horror. I couldn't be part of actually burying my mother. I told my husband not to throw dirt either because I knew he didn't like her, and he had made some comment about how it would be his pleasure to help bury her. However he meant it, it made me feel sick. Neither one of us would throw any dirt in.

We drove back home, and I really needed to lie down. The kids had come back with us. I changed out of my clothes while he and the kids were in the kitchen. When I came out, the oldest child started yelling that he hated me. He said I didn't think he was good enough to ride to the funeral with me. He was twelve. Where do you think that notion came from? I was past numb and couldn't even address it. I went to my room and took a nap. A couple of hours later we had to be at my parents' house for the first night of Shiva. I don't think the kids were with us for that. I think they went back to their mother's house. We got there before people showed up for the service. My dad and my sister were having some kind of fight. I didn't know about what. Did it matter? Couldn't we act like a caring family? Better yet, SHOULDN'T we act like a caring family? My husband was out on the front steps with his friends, smoking a cigarette. I was inside, numb and dazed, mostly on autopilot. There were lots of people that showed up. I looked up, and there was my dad standing by himself. I didn't think he SHOULD have to stand alone. So I took two or three steps forward and put my arms around him, leaving my husband with his friends. Again, it was all so surreal, the reason we were there and how I was treated by my husband the day of my mother's funeral. My autopilot is probably not any different than anyone else's. I talked to a lot of people, thanked them for coming to the service, thanked them for caring but not remembering things moment to moment. After all the people left, I stayed for a bit. Then I really was exhausted and asked to go home. We got in the car and my husband asked, "How could you humiliate me that way in front of my friends?" I honestly didn't have a clue what he was so upset about or even what he was talking about. I asked him to explain. He said he was humiliated because I had walked away from him to go stand with my dad. I just couldn't believe this was an issue for him, or at all for that matter. I did what I thought I SHOULD have done, as I had done for him when his mom died. I put my feelings and thoughts aside and stood by them both when they needed me. This was a nightmare.

I knew there were a few more days of the Shiva. How was I going to get through this? I just couldn't seem to get out from under the hostility. How was this marriage going to survive? But as we all know, life goes on, even after a friend or family member dies. It doesn't seem fair, but life keeps moving forward. A couple of weeks went by, and the numbness started to ease a bit. Three weeks went by, and my husband came home and informed me he was going to Chicago on a business trip, and he wanted me moved out by the time he got back. I had a week to find a place to live. I had thought about staying in the house and asking him to leave, but honestly I had no fight left in me. My thoughts turned to the kids. They had already been through one divorce. I decided to leave and take nothing but my clothes, shoes, and personal items. I didn't want the kids to look at an empty space where the couch used to be and think about the divorce. I asked my dad if I could move into the basement of his house until I could find a place. He said no. So I ended up moving into a condo with one of my soon-to-be ex-husband's cousins. She was looking for a renter, and she lived in our same neighborhood. My soon-to-be ex wouldn't allow me to take both cats, so they were split up too. He only really liked the one he wanted to keep.

The divorce process was awful. All I wanted to do was get it over with. I didn't fight for any value I had put into the house. His attorney contacted me and offered me two years of alimony. I said fine.

Since we were in the same neighborhood, the kids would ride their bikes over so they could go swimming. I really did love them. One day the youngest was over and told me, "Daddy has a new girlfriend, and I think it's too soon, and it makes my stomach hurt." I asked him if he talked to his daddy about it. He said no. I told him he needed to say something to his daddy or mommy. I didn't need to know what was going on with his dad, but it was good that he told somebody.

After the youngest left, I called his dad. He became furious! All I said was that the youngest needed to talk to him about his girlfriend. He hung up on me. The next call I got was from the kid's mom. She and I had always gotten along. But she was furious as well. She was yelling at me about "pumping her kids for information." Never. I didn't want to take furniture so they wouldn't feel bad. Why would I do such an awful thing to them? She told me to never have contact with her kids again. I was floored. So that ended me seeing the kids unless we were at the grocery store at the same time. It didn't happen often, but it happened.

A few weeks later my soon-to-be ex called and asked me to give back his mother's Passover recipes. I told him I would copy them, but I would like a few of her original recipe cards. He blew up and hung up on me. The next thing I know the phone rings, and it was the oldest son calling and asking for his grandmother's recipes. I told him no problem. I would make copies so we could all have them, and I would drop them off. He said, "No, you'll give us all of the originals because you're not family, and you don't count anymore."

It was as if someone had sucked all the air out of the room. My ears started to ring. He just kept repeating how I didn't matter anymore. I lost my temper and heard myself say, "Look, you little shit, how dare you say that I don't matter." I couldn't believe it; I had finally lost my filter. I felt terrible. I hung up the phone and lay on the floor sobbing uncontrollably. I knew I SHOULDN'T have said what I said. I felt guilty, ashamed, devastated, and oh so hurt. The sobbing was out of control. I began to sound like a howling wolf. His father called, and then his mother called to tear me to shreds. Too late, I was already tearing myself to shreds. I knew this child would not speak to me for a long time. Somewhere in my mind I thought he'd figure out he was used like a pawn in a chess game easily sacrificed by us all. But I also knew he'd figure it out. He would call me in ten years or so to talk about it. But until then, I was *persona non grata*.

The divorce went on. Not a lot of negotiating. I simply acquiesced to whatever he wanted. Meanwhile, I bought a condo in his cousin's building and started life anew. At some point, my dad wanted his wheelbarrow back. My ex-to-be had it in his garage. I walked over to his house, knocked on the door, and asked him to return it. He told me to get off his property. He later put the wheelbarrow on the curb and called me to come get it. I don't remember if I picked the wheelbarrow up or if my dad did. All I know is that the sheriff's department arrived at my door and served me with a restraining order. He had told the sheriff's office that I was following and menacing him. I would be at the same grocery store he was at (it was three to four blocks from both of our places). He didn't tell them he was coming over to my condo asking to get back together just weeks before. He didn't mention that he spent a couple of nights at my place telling me he loved me (of course while he was seeing this other woman). The sheriff came in to talk to me. I was crying. I couldn't believe he would do this. What purpose did this serve? The sheriff told me that he could tell who the liars are. He had been doing this for a long time. Just by the shock on my face, he knew I hadn't done anything, but he had to serve the restraining order anyway. The sheriff and I would run into each other periodically. I think we went to the same hairdresser. I guess the restraining order didn't cover when we had to meet for our Ghet (Jewish Divorce). We had to do some ritualistic walking around each other so we could be divorced in Israel. The regular divorce was official, but honestly, I didn't want us to be on record as being married anywhere, including Israel. When all the rituals were done, it was official. We were divorced…everywhere.

I got in my car and totally broke down crying. It was just too much. In five months we had lost his mom, his aunt, our dog, my mother, and our marriage. Yes, I said five months. It was overwhelming. He came up to the window of my car and knocked. He asked me if I was OK. Did I want to come over and talk, and I did. It was really over, thank G-d. By the way, he married that woman he was seeing. They've since divorced. He's now looking for ex-wife no. 4. In fact, when my dad died, he was calling me from another state trying to convince me to get back together. It was only a few weeks, and I realized he hadn't changed a bit, but I had. I could see his BS from two thousand miles away.

Although I wasn't divorced yet, I was trying to move on with my life. I had met someone, and we were just beginning to date. I was returning a movie to the video store, and I heard someone call my name. I turned around and there was the former manager of a salon I worked at. We stood and talked for a while. It was nice to catch up with him. He was probably one of the most handsome men I had ever seen. I was walking away, and he asked me if I would like to go out to dinner when he got back from his trip. I said yes, and we exchanged phone numbers. I was pretty excited. I hadn't been out on a date in a long time. My divorce was almost final. The timing was good. He called me from out of town. I was thrilled! And so began our relationship. He took me out to dinner. He was such a gentleman. He made me laugh; he brought me flowers once a week. I liked that he wasn't rushing me into bed. I liked this "slow moving, getting to know each other" thing.

A few months went by. He was in and out of town traveling for business. I got a call one night, and he said when he got back he'd like to sit down and have a talk. I said sure. I got off the phone and tried to figure out what that was all about. I narrowed it down to two things. Either he was ready to tell me that he loved me or he was going to tell me he had herpes and wanted to be open and honest about it. I can honestly tell you I was prepared for either. I could see myself falling in love with him and having a long-term relationship, and I felt bad for him having to tell me the latter because I had to have that conversation myself thanks to my relationship with the stripper. It's really difficult to conjure up the courage to tell someone you're "damaged" in any way, but a sexually transmitted disease? There's no good way to tell anyone. So I waited until he was back.

He came over to my house. I made dinner, and he was oddly quiet. Poor guy. I was pretty sure which of the "either/or" it was. But I couldn't say it for him. After dinner we sat staring at each other. He finally spoke after a lot of hemming and hawing. It was tough to watch him find just the right words. But I knew he needed to tell me in his own way, in his own time. He told me how much he liked sharing time with me, but he had something he had to say. He wanted to be honest so I would have a choice. Well, now I knew for sure! He said, "I have herpes. I've had it for a while. I got it from a former girlfriend many years ago. I want to tell you so you could choose to have a physical relationship with me." I took a breath and said, "Welcome to the club." He started to laugh and said, "What? You're kidding." Nope, not kidding. From there it was full speed ahead. He was a kind, caring, and a gentle lover. It was a nice loving relationship. I can honestly say he provided me with my most romantic and dreamy evening, sexually and otherwise. It hadn't happened before, and twenty years later, that feeling hasn't happened since. Too bad because challenges were about to get in the way of what could have been a happy ending.

When a man is prettier than you and takes longer than you do in the bathroom to get ready, run! This SHOULD be a really good indicator of what's the most important thing in this man's life. He always had perfect hair. I admired that about him. He was always impeccably groomed.

We started out strong. I thought I had found a decent one at last! I liked that we had a life together, but we also had a life apart from one another. He had his own friends and interests; I had mine.

I thought it was sweet that he decided to get allergy shots so he could be around my cats.

It was about three months into the relationship, and everything was going smoothly. One night we went to the hospital to see a friend of mine. Afterward I dropped him off at his apartment. He said he was tired, and I had plans to go out with a girlfriend. I'm not sure if we were saying the "love" word yet, but I certainly let him know that I cared about him. I called him before I went out and there was no answer. I figured he must have been in the shower or something. My girlfriend and I went out as planned and got home about 1:30 a.m. I checked for messages on my voice mail and found a peculiar message from "my man." He was saying something about me not being where I said I would be. After listening to the message, I realized he was drunk. So begins the downward slide. I called him back, and he started accusing me of the craziest things. What was I doing—or should he rephrase—"who" was I doing? Why I would take it upon myself to try to talk sense into someone three sheets to the wind is beyond me. I guess it's that training I've referred to before. I thought I could fix things. There really wasn't anything to be fixed, but I was going to fix it. I actually tried to talk sense into him until 4:00 a.m. I finally realized he wasn't sobering up at all; it just seemed to get worse. I told him I wasn't going to discuss it anymore, and we would talk at a later date.

I went to bed for a few hours, then got going early that morning. I had turned my mobile phone on in case someone needed me while I was running errands. My phone rang. Guess who? He wanted to know if I was still talking to him. I told him I wasn't very happy, and I was not up to dealing with this kind of problem. He said he needed to talk to me in person. I agreed to meet him for lunch. Sheepish is an understatement. I've never seen a man so sorry. I told him in no uncertain terms how I felt about drug and alcohol problems and was not up to dealing with it. Been there, done that! He said it wouldn't happen again. The problem, as I saw it, was not just the fact he went out drinking, he went out drinking alone and drove home drunk. I wasn't very fond of the tone he took with me, nor the accusations he made when he left me the voice mail. He kept apologizing. I asked him to come back to my house so we could talk some more. When we got there, I cued up his voice-mail message he had left me in his drunken stupor and made him listen to it. See, there is method to my madness. He turned all red and apologized some more. He said he was thinking about going to AA. A week later, he decided he could help himself, and he would not drink for a while. Two weeks later, we went to a restaurant and he ordered a glass of wine. He looked at me as if I said something. He started rationalizing about wine not being hard liquor, and it was OK, and I wasn't going to tell him what to do. Mind you, I never said anything. He sat there obviously feeling guilty he ordered the wine and let it sit there and never drank it. Then he basically blamed it on me because I supposedly gave him a dirty look. Can you say "Trouble in Paradise"?

My womanly training told me to make this work. I tried; he tried. Things got a little better. He was still drinking, but he just didn't do it around me, or at least not too much. One night we were going to bed. He was on his side, he got up and walked around my side of the bed and got down on one knee. I panicked! I started asking him what he was doing. He looked down at his posture and started to laugh and just kept repeating oh, no, no, no. I told him never to scare me like that again. We had talked about what it would be like to get married. But it was all hypothetical. He had talked about buying me this ring he had seen. It ended up causing us one of the biggest fights we ever had. I'm not sure why. In retrospect, I figure it must have been because I knew it would never work in a million years. Like I said, "Trouble in Paradise."

Things just kept getting worse. All the things we found endearing about each other got really annoying. I was unhappy, so was he. He called me one night to tell me he was going out with his friends. I told him to drive carefully, better yet, not to drive at all, take a cab. He assured me he wasn't going to be drinking enough to worry about his blood alcohol level. I didn't hear from him until two days later. It turns out he was picked up for DWI, and he didn't want to call anyone to get him out of jail, so he just stayed there. He had to go to court, where they sentenced him to five days in the workhouse and Mothers Against Drunk Drivers classes. They suspended his license for I can't remember how long. You'd think a person would learn. This was not the first time in the workhouse for the same reason. When he got out, he couldn't drive anywhere. If I wanted to see him, I had to go pick him up, unless he was being stubborn and insisted on walking in the below zero temperatures. Oh, well, maybe something would teach him a lesson.

When I saw him the first night after he got out of the workhouse, all he did was tell me how uncomfortable the pillows were, how bad the food was, and how loud and strange the people were in jail. I told him I couldn't feel very sorry for him because it wasn't supposed to be a five-star hotel. Can you say, "On the way to a breakup"? We're coming into the final stretch of the last straw. Now the two of us had more problems than this. I will be the first to admit I expect respect and if I don't get it, I lose patience really easily. I give respect; I SHOULD get respect, right? Fat chance. That is the thing dreams are made of. Back to the story.

I went to pick him up one night so he could come over for a while. He was kind of pissy in the car, but I chose to ignore it. We got back to the house and cuddled up on the couch. Things were strained but seemed to be getting better. We ended up in bed trying to make love. I had to be very specific; he was very distant but interested. That probably doesn't make any sense, but that's the way it was. He was standing behind me, I could see him in the mirror, and the strangest thing came to mind. He looked like a perfect crescent moon. I couldn't get that thought out of my mind during this short-lived encounter. When he was done he said, "Is that what you wanted?" As if this was all my idea. After that statement, I told him I would take him home, knowing that was the last time we would be together. The good thing about that relationship was I found out I could have deep feelings for someone or something other than my cats.

In my twenties, I discovered my sexual freedom. I could have sex with abandon. No judgments, just adventure. I had anxiety about so many things. Sex was not one of them. I became experienced, whatever that means. I thought everyone felt that sex was a way of expressing yourself, relieving tension, blowing off steam, if you will. Not necessarily an "intimacy." As I've said, sex was challenging in my marriage. After my divorce, I thought that freedom would reintroduce itself to me. That's not really the way things happened. After my one serious relationship broke up (the one after my divorce), I tried to get back to my old ways, sex without the intimacy. Maybe I had changed. Maybe the times had changed. But I still wanted sex to be fun. I was meeting men; I even had sex with a couple of them. It was not as much fun as I remembered.

Then I met one who would become my next boyfriend. We had grown up in the same neighborhood. We started dating. We seemed to get along just fine. One thing led to another, and a few months into dating, we slept together. I broke a rule I had. Do not ever spend the night with anybody without having my car with me. We had gone out for a lovely dinner, then back to his apartment. Things started off OK. Then I realized he wasn't paying any attention to what was going on with my body. He seemed to be on autopilot. I could have been any number of women. I had never had that happen before. But I went with it, thinking things would get better. Then "we" were done. He fell asleep. I wanted to go home. I had no car. I considered calling a cab, but I called my best friend instead. I cried to her about what happened. Wasn't sex supposed to be fun? I tried to think of this as being a "new" thing. I SHOULD probably try this again after I had a conversation with this man. I liked him, but I couldn't imagine being in a relationship where there was going to be bad sex. As I was talking to my friend, he had awakened and walked into the room I was sitting in. I hung up my phone and told him we needed to talk about what just happened. I was very frank with him. I told him that things started out OK, and then he became distant, almost seeming like he was on autopilot. This was back in the day when Andrew Dice Clay was at his prime as a comedian. He has used the word "cum catcher" in his act. That was how Andrew Dice Clay described his casual sexual encounters. Nothing I could have ever thought of myself, but was an accurate description of how I felt. I knew that this man and I were not casual. As far as I knew, we were building a relationship. In the middle of sex, he emotionally checked out. I felt hurt somehow. We talked for quite some time. He apologized, and then he took me home. He said he still wanted to go out and make it up to me. SHOULDN'T I give him a second chance? Of course I SHOULD.

We continued to see each other for another six months or so. Every time we had sex, I doubted that sex was supposed to be fun anymore. Maybe we were "at an age" that sex isn't fun? How is that possible? At that six-month mark, he took me to a party where people were watching college basketball championships. His friends seemed nice enough. I wasn't a basketball fan and ended up talking to some women in the kitchen who didn't care if they saw the game either. It was a nice evening. Two days later he broke up with me totally out of the blue. I was shocked! He told me he had to break up with me because he was ashamed and embarrassed to bring me around his friends because he didn't know how to explain me. I had not gone to college and that seemed to be a problem for him. The other problem was that I didn't have any money. What? So he came over and got what few things he had left at my place. But he thought it would be nice if he gave me his Basia CD. So the moral of this story is: Sex is supposed to be fun and compatible. Some men are shallow and idiots. But on the up side, I have Basia CD—really the best thing about the whole relationship…sad, but true. By the way, he went on to marry an attorney. Evidently she had the appropriate credentials. I wish them well.

It would be many years before I would get into another relationship. They hadn't served me very well in the past. Why do it again? Out of the blue, I started thinking about this guy I met when I was in junior high. We had run into each other in various places around the city for years and years. Every time we'd see each other, one or both of us would be involved in a relationship, or one or both of us were married. I started wondering what happened to him. I called his cousin. His cousin told me he was single and living in Arizona. SHOULD I dare call him? Of course I SHOULD. I got his voice mail. I left a message. Within a day I heard back. He seemed very happy to hear from me. We started talking every day, sometimes twice a day. He told me he was thinking about moving back here soon. He just had to work out some things about the custody of his son with his ex-wife. Months went by, and he decided to fly up to see me. It was all so exciting! His friends had picked him up at the airport. They had gone out to dinner and then dropped him off at my place. I would meet all of them, along with seeing this guy I hadn't seen in years. No pressure at all!

I remember walking out to the car while repeating in my head, "Don't trip, don't fall, don't trip, don't fall." He got out of the car and looked as cute as I had remembered. We hugged, and he introduced me to the gang. He had a suitcase with him. We said good-bye to his friends and walked inside. I knew as soon as I saw him I was in love with him. I had a crush on him in junior high, but this was love. I was sure of it. All the times we had run into each other and one or both of us weren't available…this was love! He felt like the yin to my yang. Our styles matched up, our humor matched up, our passion matched up. How could it not be true love?

For the first few months he would fly back and forth. Most of the time I paid for his tickets, as he was looking for a job. I even got him an interview with a friend of mine here. He was thinking of moving from Arizona. Why not move in with me? It made a lot of sense at the time. He interviewed and got the job. He was in town in September 2001. On September 10, 2001, he and I went out to dinner with my dad and stepmother. During dinner he asked my dad if he could marry me. It was all so exciting! We had been out shopping and had looked at rings. We picked one out together, and I used my mother's diamond to put in the setting. We were waiting for the jeweler to set it. My dad and stepmother were very excited. My dad said, of course! Then we celebrated our engagement with them. My fiancé (without the ring) and I went home, and we sat in a candlelit bath and talked about our future together.

The next day was September 11, 2001. Yes, that September 11. He was supposed to fly home that day, but as we all know, all air travel was suspended for four days. I SHOULD have known that one disaster would follow another. Sorry for being so glib. He was angry he couldn't get back to Arizona to see his son. He didn't understand what flying west had to do with what was happening on the East Coast. The whole thing was surreal. An attack on American soil? Who would have thought that could happen? But all the concern for him was focused on why he couldn't fly. I told him to call his five-year-old son and explain to him that the President of the United States said he couldn't fly home. That was the best explanation he could give. For four days he paced and carried on. I understood the frustration of not being able to do what he needed to do, but this was a national security issue. I remember thinking the silence of no planes flying over was deafening. Finally, the ban was lifted, and he flew back to Arizona to start preparing for his move here. It was hard to gauge my anxiety. It seemed to match up with the country's anxiety. I don't think I could have put the pieces together of how significant his reaction was to not being able to leave.

Several weeks later, we began our life together. I had a two-bedroom, one-bathroom condo in the suburbs. It was a little tough integrating his stuff in with mine, but I was more than happy to do it. We settled in nicely together. We spent time with his and my friends. Just about everyone loved us together. A couple of my friends were a little skeptical, but they went with it. He was quite charming, sweet, and funny. I felt I was in the healthiest relationship I had ever been in. We seemed to communicate really well. We did all those "couple" things together. We went to the coffee shop on Sunday morning before we would go shopping at Costco. We met friends for dinners and breakfasts. We worked hard at our respective jobs. I seemed to be paying a little bit more than he was, but for me that was OK until he got settled.

About a year went by, and he came home from work and wanted to talk. We sat down on the couch, and he told me he felt really bad that he wasn't contributing enough financially to our household. He thought maybe he should move out so he wouldn't be a burden. As odd as I thought that statement was, I assured him he wasn't a burden and that I was sure work for him would pick up. I wasn't worried. He asked me if I was sure. I said, of course. That's what couples do, support each other during tough times.

We continued to live together in what I thought was a happy relationship. My engagement ring was ready, so we went together to pick it up. It was beautiful. It was gold and the crown was made of hearts that the diamond set into. I showed my ring to my sister and all she could say was, "Good thing that's not my ring. I hate hearts." She was right, good thing.

As plans for the wedding started taking shape, I suggested that he and I talk to our Rabbi for premarital screening. I had already been through one divorce; he had been through three. (No red flags there). I didn't want the same mistakes that had happened to us in the past, happen again. We made an appointment and started seeing the Rabbi once a week. The Rabbi suggested we talk to a psychologist that dealt with premarital issues. It all made perfect sense to me. My fiancé had started acting kind of erratically. Happy one day, not so happy the next day. It was odd to watch. I would try to talk to him about it, but he had no comment.

We were supposed to go out to lunch with a friend of my fiancé's. As we were pulling up to the restaurant, he asked me to take the ring off and put it in my pocket. What? He said he hadn't told his friends yet, and he didn't want to be teased by them because he was getting married again. What? I begrudgingly took off my ring (that I had paid for, by the way) and put it in my pocket. Red flag! We went to lunch with his friend, and nothing was mentioned about our engagement or any of our plans, for that matter. I asked for an explanation when we got home. He said he chickened out of telling him. He was so sorry. Could I forgive him? I didn't know what to say. I knew I would bring it up in counseling.

The next night we were invited to one of my girlfriend's birthday parties. He and I were getting ready to go, and all of a sudden he started a fight. I don't know about what, but I remember saying to him, "This is smoke from a distant fire. It has nothing to do with me." The next thing he did was pick up a small dish from the kitchen table and throw it directly at my head! I ducked, and it missed me. Everything for me was kind of blank after that. I know we ended up going to that party. I was shaken up and really confused. I was standing talking to some people, and he came up behind me and put his arms around me and told me how much he loved me. He started telling the people around us how much we loved each other. I just stood there, trying to process what was happening. I was blank about everything after that until we got home. I asked him why he was behaving that way. He had no answer. He told me he was going to bed. He went into our room and closed the door and promptly went to sleep. I, on the other hand, stayed up all night with a yellow legal pad divided into two columns, one "pro," one "con." I wrote down things in both columns, but the "con" column won.

As soon as the clock struck 9:00 a.m., I went in to our room, woke him up, and told him he had to move out. I told him we SHOULD continue to talk to the counselor. Maybe separately we could work things out. But I would not allow anyone to throw something at my head and treat me so disrespectfully. He got up, took his time, called his friends, and arranged to move his stuff, including the dresser I bought for him. By that night, he was gone. By that night, I was heartbroken.

We continued to talk on the phone every other day. The strange thing was, I wanted to work things out; he just wanted me to buy him things. Our counseling appointment was coming up, and he agreed to go, at least one last time. While we were in session I said to the psychologist, "Either he is bipolar, or he is a con man." The psychologist asked me why I had to "label" what was happening. I said, "Because my behavior hasn't changed at all, his has." He became angry. She tried to get him to talk about his anger but to no avail.

About two weeks later his cellular phone bill arrived. I looked at the outside of the envelope and then threw it on the floor. I stared at it for hours. I finally somehow rationalized in my head that I was paying for his phone, and because it was on my account, I could look at his bill. I had never opened anyone else's mail. But I just had to. I opened it and there was a number that he was calling over and over again. Seventy-two minutes for one call, fifty-four minutes for another. There were twenty-four calls he made to that number. That only said one thing to me; he was cheating.

It was about midnight by the time I opened that envelope. I logged on to my computer and Googled the number. Up popped her picture. She looked a lot like me. So now I had her name. I knew I would wait until morning to call her. At 8:00 a.m. I called her. I told her that I had found her number a couple of times on my cell phone bill, and I just wanted to verify that it wasn't a wrong number. She told me her name and what she did for a living. I told her it didn't sound familiar, and I should probably call my cell phone company and have the charges removed. "Oh," I said, "there could be one other possibility. Do you know [my fiancé's name]?" She said, "Yes, I do." I asked her if they had been sleeping together. She said she thought I should ask him. In other words, yes. I introduced myself as his fiancé. And she said, "Well, don't break up with him on account of me. I've met someone I like better." Wow! She said they had met on a popular dating website. I thanked her and hung up the phone. I proceeded to sob uncontrollably and call in sick to work. I went on that popular dating website and found his profile. Not only did he say he was single, he used my pets as bait. He used a picture of himself that was ten years old. The whole profile was full of lies. In fact, it was sickeningly ironic in parts. I just couldn't believe it. He must have been setting up online dating while I was sleeping. I called a friend to come over and sit with me. I calmed down and called the Rabbi and canceled all wedding plans as well as calling our counselor and letting her know we wouldn't need her services anymore. It was an awful day!

The upside, we hadn't ordered wedding invitations yet. The downside, I had already bought a wedding dress. I spent the next weeks getting rid of anything having to do with the wedding. I took the dress and a bracelet into a consignment store. I took my ring in and had it melted and had the diamond set into a custom-designed ring. I had a lot of support from all my friends. I sat in my own therapist's office and sobbed. He told me he was proud of me for seeing the problems before we got married. He told me I was brave in asking my fiancé to move out. I really considered it a bullet well-dodged. But it would take years to get over all the drama.

It was seven years before I would have another relationship. That includes no dating, no casual sex, nothing. I decided to take the time to look within to try to understand why relationships ended so badly. I really wanted to know why it seemed I picked the wrong men all of the time. During those seven years, I had an ongoing friendship with a man. In fact, I called him "better than a boyfriend." We went out for dinner, went to movies, went shopping, and just generally hung out. No sex. He helped me through my break up with my fiancé. I cried; he listened. I vented; he offered advice. I talked him through a couple of breakups of his own. It was a wonderful supportive friendship.

About year six of our friendship, my friends started asking me why we weren't dating. I kept saying, "Because he's better than a boyfriend." Then he sat down with me one day and asked me if we could move our friendship to the next level. He said he wanted to try to have a relationship with me. I told him I didn't know if I was willing to lose our friendship if our relationship ended badly. Honestly, that conversation went on for a year. We'd talk about it all the time. My gut told me we'd lose our friendship if we started dating.

Finally I acquiesced. He had built a good case for our friendship being so strong that we couldn't possibly ever lose our connection. So we started dating exclusively. We were a couple. It was odd but natural. I know that makes no sense at all. Things were going pretty well. We finally slept together. That felt strange to me. But we were changing the dynamic of our life together, so I chalked it up to that. Our communication was changing. He didn't seem to be as clear with what he wanted from our relationship as he was when he made such a good case for us to change from being friends to lovers. I tried to pay attention to the details of his wants and needs. He had very specific fetishes that were fun. But I also noted that he seemed to have a lot of shame or guilt around having sex. I figured we'd work through that too. But it made things very difficult for me. I was having my own issues regarding sex after menopause. My body didn't work the same as it did years prior. After seven years of no sex, that was troublesome for me. But we were going to work through all these issues. I did not want to fail at this relationship.

I started noticing that he wasn't very sensitive or helpful when it came to me having a cold or the flu. I could feel myself starting to reassess this whole thing. But I soldiered on. We had been together as a couple for about nine or ten months when he called me a couple of days before my birthday to let me know he had talked to his accountant about marrying me. What? He wanted his accountant to tell him if it would be financially sound to marry me. The odd thing was, he had never talked to me about marrying me. I said to him, "Did it ever occur to you to ask me if I wanted to get married?" He didn't say anything to that; he just went on telling me what his accountant had said. I sat there shaking my head. I knew this was the beginning of the end of our relationship and probably our friendship as well. I knew I had to talk to him about his insensitivity, his priorities, and his thought process.

We went out for my birthday a couple of days later, and I tried, really I did. But he was distant. In fact, he was checking his work texts during dinner. I had gotten used to his dedication to his work life for all the time we were friends. He got called away often. But he couldn't even take the time to pick up my birthday present. He called me to go pick it up and told me he had paid for it over the phone. After dinner we tried to have sex, but it just didn't work. He left my house and went home. I was sick to my stomach. So many other little things had happened, and I realized that he wasn't going to be the person he said he would be. He wanted me to be a convenient part of his life. He didn't want to sacrifice any work time, and he didn't want to sacrifice any of his time unless it didn't cut into other things he wanted to do.

I called him the next day, and he didn't answer his phone. I left a message, and he didn't return my call. I was hoping this wasn't another one of his disappearing acts. (Before we were a couple, he would disappear for days. He wouldn't pick up his phone or return calls. As his friend, I asked him not to do that because it just caused me to worry that something was wrong). After many hours went by with no call, I texted him and asked if we could go to dinner. He texted me back saying, "Text me your agenda." What? The only way he would communicate with me was via text. He wanted me to text him any questions I had for him, and he would evaluate them and text me back the answers. I'm telling you, I can't make this stuff up! I asked him via text to call me. He texted back again, "Text me your agenda." I texted back, "I am not a business meeting; I'm your girlfriend." He kept texting about my "agenda." I finally gave up and that's how our relationship ended. I was stunned; my friends were stunned! No one could figure out what happened. It was just…over.

About six months later, he contacted me and asked if I wanted to meet him for breakfast. I thought it would be the perfect opportunity to find out what happened. He really never answered the question about what happened. We talked about trying to rebuild our friendship. That's what I missed the most—our friendship. I SHOULD have listened to my gut. It was screaming not to have a relationship with him, that our friendship was just fine. But he assured me we'd be OK. I believed him. I tried to believe in us, as a couple. We had breakfast a couple more times, and I realized our friendship had suffered too big of a blow. My trust in him was gone.

But because I am who I am, there were lessons to be learned from that relationship. That will be discussed in another chapter.

CHAPTER 10

Wicked Steps

Before my mother died, she told me not to give my dad a hard time when he started dating. She had told him he had to wait six months because that would be a respectable amount of time to grieve. She had also told him the three women he couldn't date or she would come back to haunt him.

The "respectable" amount of time went by. Dad had been dating. Little did I know what all of that entailed. Probably a good thing, but I'll get to that later.

I was out shopping at the local Target store and ran into my dad. While we were talking, a woman around my dad's age whom we both knew walked up and started talking to us. It wasn't a long conversation. After she walked away my dad said, "I think I'm going to ask her out." And so began the courtship to my dad's second marriage. She had three sons; two were married with children. They were all in the entertainment business.

As things progressed, we all started spending time together. I can honestly say that the first few times were not entirely comfortable for me. But this wasn't about me; it was about my dad being happy. Her kids seemed very nice. They all seemed excited to have new potential "family" members. Was this the family I was always looking for? Wouldn't that be wonderful?

After several months, Dad and this woman got engaged. They asked all of us what we thought about them just living together without getting married. It was more about their individual social security payments, etcetera. We all gave our blessing to them to not get married. A few months went by, and they set a date to be married. They thought they SHOULD marry because they were from "that era." I asked this woman to join me for lunch so we could have a private talk. I wanted to be completely candid with her. I told her I thought it was great that she and my dad had found each other and were getting married. I wanted them to be happy together. But I didn't know how she was going to fit into my life, other than as a friend. At thirty-seven years old, I wasn't looking for another mother. I told her I may be a "pill" until I figured it out. But as long as she and Dad were happy, all was right with the world. I think she was a bit taken aback but understood where I was coming from.

The wedding plans were set in motion. They got married at a relative's house. It was a beautiful outdoor wedding. One of her sons walked her down the aisle. They said their vows, and my dad cried.

I really don't remember much. I remember there were a lot of bees. We were now officially *The Brady Bunch*. She had three sons; Dad had two daughters. There were spouses and grandkids on both sides, except for me. No kids, no spouse. What a great clan to be family with! Right? Whoa, hold up. Here's the rest of the story, "Paul Harvey."

After they got married, there were a lot of family gatherings—every Jewish holiday, birthdays, anniversaries. I was happy to show up and more than happy to cook and clean up. I was always at these events with a smile on my face, waiting to bond as a family. The thing was, it wasn't happening. It wasn't for my lack of trying. Oh, have I mentioned who one of the "family" members was? One of the "mean girls" from my high school days—one who tormented me daily. But now we were almost forty. Surely things would be different now, right? No, she hadn't changed a bit. That was when I realized why the bonding wasn't happening. For me this was like being in high school all over again. "They" were the "popular kids"; I was the outsider...again.

My sister didn't bother showing up to these family things at all. I was miserable around these people. But I was going to keep trying. Besides, I thought I SHOULD because someone should represent Dad's side of the family. Mom had said, "Don't give your dad a hard time."

Jewish holidays were particularly bad. There are so many stories. Let me start with Rosh Hashanah in 2001 or 2002. The year doesn't really matter. I got a call from my stepbrother's wife, asking if I would make and bring a turkey for Rosh Hashanah dinner. Well, with my history of turkey schlepping, that wasn't a problem. If I'm not mistaken, I had a twenty-five-pound turkey for fifteen people. So I cleaned, roasted, basted, and schlepped the turkey over to her house. I brought the turkey into the kitchen, and what do I see? Another cooked turkey! I asked, "I thought you were making a brisket?" She said she did, but she felt like making a turkey too. Needless to say, I was a bit confused. She could have called me and said, "Never mind on the turkey thing." I can tell you it made me uncomfortable. I didn't know why. But it gave me a feeling of dread. So I put my turkey on the center island and started helping around the kitchen. I turned around, and my stepbrother had a piece of my turkey in his hand and was taking a bite. Right in front of his wife he says, "I don't know what you do to your turkey, but it's better than my wife's." The look on her face made me freeze. I started hearing that PTSD ringing in my ears. I wanted to turn and run away. I managed to walk up to my stepbrother and quietly say to him, "Do you ever want to get laid again?" For me I felt a bit out of body. Time seemed to crawl by. About ten minutes later, his wife walks over and asks me to step out into the hallway away from everyone. She said to me, "Don't you ever bring another turkey over here again." Then she walked away and back in with everyone. I know she wasn't kidding with me. She was pissed! Why at me and not at her husband? I can't answer that. But I did get the impression if this were any "other" kind of "family," I would have been sleeping with the fishes.

Another Jewish holiday, Yom Kippur, we were breaking the fast at a different brother's house. I had learned from past gatherings that if I just kept moving, it was harder to hit a moving target. I would set tables, set up buffets, clear dishes, rinse dishes, wrap leftovers, anything to keep me from sitting down for long periods of time. I had helped all I could, and a bunch of us sat down at the kitchen table, including me. My dad, his wife, my stepbrother, and his wife and sister–in-law were all sitting there talking. I'm not sure what led the conversation in the direction it took, but I do know I tried to stop it. My stepbrother brought up the subject of who my dad dated before my dad married his mother. I was immediately on alert, but somehow I couldn't move to get up from the table. So my dad started talking about a couple of women he dated. He mentioned this woman who used to be a neighbor of ours. I was surprised. I never knew he went out with her. My stepbrother's next question about this particular woman was, "So did you bone her?" My sight went blurry; my ears started to ring. I was horrified by the question. I looked at my stepbrother and said, "I would rather blow my head off than hear the answer to that question." I looked at both my dad and his wife. They looked uncomfortable. He asked again, "So did you bone her?" And in front of G-d and everyone, my dad started talking about how he had slept with her, gave some details, and laughed as did my stepbrother. My dad's wife didn't seem amused. I got up and left. I cried all the way home. For me it felt like a violation of sorts, more inappropriate behavior. I was sick to my stomach. I started begging out of dinners periodically after that.

Years later I decided to host a combo Rosh Hashanah/anniversary dinner. It was Dad and his wife's tenth anniversary. I thought that I would have a bit more control of inappropriate behavior if I hosted. What was I thinking? I was going to have the dinner in the party room at my apartment building. No one would have to be in my actual apartment. I started planning about three weeks in advance. People started calling, asking if they could help. I delegated items. Everything seemed to be going smoothly until a few days before the dinner. Everyone that said they were going to do something either wanted to change what they were doing or bringing, didn't know if they would be able to show up, or invited extra people. You've heard the term: "Like herding cats?" Well, I have cats. They're easier to deal with. I had ordered a cake for my dad and his wife's anniversary. I cooked many different things. I bought beautiful china-looking disposable plates, glasses, and plastic ware. I was trying to make cleanup easy. This particular Rosh Hashanah was on the night of the Minnesota Vikings first season game. I figured we'd get through the short service before dinner and then turn on the game. In the party room was a new TV and sound system. There were specific instructions on how to get everything to work properly. I had said, let's get the service part over with, and then we can turn on the game.

So as I'm setting up the buffet, I hear the TV go on. The "kids" were messing with all the remotes. I asked them to turn the TV off until the service was over. No one was listening to me. My dad's wife told me to "lighten up." Never would I go into someone else's house and tell them what to do. What made it worse was—stay with me—you have to picture an old-fashioned game of musical chairs. I had set up two long tables because so many people were coming to dinner. It turned out, a lot of them didn't show up. When dinner started, all of the "popular kids" ran for the same table, some even taking chairs and place settings from the other table. Sound like high school lunchroom to you? Every single one of my "extended" family was rude that night, including my dad's wife. I was appalled by everyone's behavior. Notice I said appalled and not surprised. Why SHOULD I be surprised? This was nothing new. This was just an amped up level of rudeness.

We went from Rosh Hashanah prayers to the football game (which was on during the prayers) to the anniversary celebration for my dad and his wife. The cake I had ordered was on a separate small table with flowers on it. We had to listen to yet another one of my dad's wife's poems with all of its disingenuous BS. I have never been so glad to see people leave in my life. I finished cleaning up and swore to myself I would never host another dinner for them again.

The next day I got a call from my dad's wife. She wanted to thank me for all of my hard work...but...she thought I spent too much money making the room look nice. I SHOULD have kept things more simple. I SHOULDN'T have made so much food and that went on ad nauseam. I was already so frustrated with everyone's behavior and so disappointed in everyone's attention to Rosh

Hashanah. Now with that call, I felt disrespected, defeated, and angry. With that call, I found my voice and my backbone. I told her how I felt about everyone's behavior, including her phone call. I told her I thought her family was difficult and disrespectful of me. At that point I could honestly say I didn't care if I was at another "family" gathering again.

She became angry and told me I would not be invited to anything again. For some reason, that was fine with me. I told her she would have to explain to my dad why she wasn't going to invite me to be with him. She had spent so much time manipulating me through guilt, through mentioning my mother, through mentioning what family SHOULD be, I had had enough. I figured my dad would step up and tell her it wasn't OK for her to do that. Every gathering we had been at, whenever I was out of my dad's line of sight, I would hear him say, "Where's Roberta?" How was she going to explain that? Good luck.

Nine days after the Rosh Hashanah fiasco my dad called and told me he lost his cell phone. I told him I had an extra one and would bring it over the next morning after Yom Kippur services. The next morning I went over to drop off the phone. I walked in and there was the table already set for the break-the-fast dinner that night. I quietly counted the place settings. There was enough for everyone but me. I sat down with my dad and showed him how to use the phone. He asked if I was coming to break the fast. I told him I wasn't invited and looked straight into his wife's eyes. He looked at her too. He said nothing. Not a question, not a statement…nothing. I even waited another minute…still nothing. So I left. I ended up breaking the fast at my friend's Asian restaurant. So that was the end of me trying to please. Early on I felt that my dad's wife was manipulative. When she was telling my dad he had too much stuff from the house he had with my mom, she would ask him to give it away either to my sister and me or to some organization. I do have to admit my dad was a pack rat but not a hoarder. One day I was at their place, and she took out some items that were my mother's. I didn't want them. I didn't have room for more stuff. She held up a weighted crystal bird and said in a sing-song voice, "You SHOULD take it, it was your mother's." I took it. I don't know why. It stayed with me for a few years until I donated it to someone's fund-raiser.

My dad's wife used guilt and manipulation a lot, the worst being every Mother's Day. My mom died in 1994. I don't have any biological kids of my own. It's a "Hallmark Holiday," as far as I'm concerned. I had made it clear from the beginning that I didn't want to spend Mother's Day with her or with anyone. I wanted to plant my garden and spend time by myself. But every year she and my dad would get completely worked up about how I SHOULD want to spend Mother's Day with her. Over and over again I would explain that I don't have a mother anymore and wasn't looking for a new one. I was thirty-seven when they got married. I SHOULD be able to make these choices for myself. Every year I got harassed about it. I finally had had enough. I went to their condo to talk calmly to them about respecting my voice not to spend Mother's Day with them. They were not listening to me. I finally started crying. I told them my choice was to be left alone on Mother's Day. I didn't want any card from my dad's wife that came from my cats. I didn't want to go to brunch or dinner. In fact, I didn't want to talk to either of them on that day. They always had to bring up that my sister spent time with them on Mother's Day. I told them that was her choice, not mine.

You've probably gathered by now that my dad, his wife, and my sister had no boundaries regarding me or my life. I was doing my damnedest to set them. I left there furious. Furious that I had cried, furious they didn't think enough of me to honor my request. There are 365 days in a year. I was asking for just one to myself. I remember everything that was said that day, but I have no recollection of faces, just the lamp that sat on a table next to the couch. Even after that, they still asked me to join them every year. Every year I politely said no.

My dad asked me to go to lunch with him to talk about something. This couldn't be a good thing. After we ordered he said to me, "[My wife] says that there are no pictures of her up in your apartment, and it hurts her feelings." I just sat there in utter disbelief. Now she's going to manipulate me into putting pictures of her up in my apartment? Seriously? He continued, "Could you just put one up for me?" Boundaries! Where are the boundaries?

This was right around my dad's ninetieth birthday. She was going to throw a big party for him. I'm sure someone would be taking pictures. Sure enough, the day of the party someone took a family photo—Dad and his wife sitting in the front and the rest of us gathered around. I framed that photo and put it on a small table in the hall facing the front door so if and when they came over, it would be the first thing they saw. On the table, it was out of my sightline most of the time. Yes, a little passive-aggressive, I know!

Remember, I was now related (through Dad's marriage) to one of the "mean girls" from K-12th grade. She called and wanted to know if she could borrow some folding chairs and a folding table. I said sure, but she would have to come over and get them. When she walked in, the first thing she saw was that picture. She said, "What is that, a shrine?" I just had to chuckle. I didn't say anything. I just let the question hang in the air.

Let's just face it, my dad married another narcissist. But this one came with her own narcissistic family. Early on each of them seemed to be interested in getting to know my sister and me. But that waned when the novelty wore off for them. My sister wasn't around them much. Me, I just became "the help" again. I was always being asked to do something. Which beats the alternative, I guess. I noticed there was a lot of manipulation from my dad and his wife. In some instances it was easier to do what they wanted me to do. When I'd put my foot down and said "no, thank you," "no, I don't want to," and "no, I don't think so," my life became more difficult due to the pressure or guilt that both of them would lay on me. My dad would just stop trying to change my mind, but his wife didn't take no for an answer. One of her kids said their nickname for her was "The Bulldozer." Fitting, I thought. Another reason I did all these things with them—for them—my dad was ninety. How much longer could this go on? I know that sounds terrible, but it's honest. Why waste time fighting when time was not on my dad's side?

My dad's wife would ask me what it was like growing up with my mom and dad. At first I would just say, "It was difficult at best." She would press me for some details. I finally told her my mom and dad were abusive. After finding that out, she would jokingly say in front of her whole family, "They grew up like the Von Trapp family." I just found that minimization infuriating. After she had said it for years and for the umpteenth time, I finally said, "We didn't sing." It got very quiet after that. I know that my abuse at the hands of my parents was no joke. She really was no better because she was equally as cruel and dismissive. In fact, she and my sister were and are "peas in a pod."

After Dad got sick for the last time and was hospitalized, I was preparing myself for the onslaught of misery. All of her children were in town for a party. I decided to beg out and stay at the hospital with my dad. I didn't want to be with all of them anyway. My sister and her husband went to the party as well. While sitting with my dad, watching football, he suddenly started to choke and was not able to breathe. The nurse came in and vacuumed out his throat and lungs. Very scary for sure. The nurses got him settled down. He was back to being able to breathe. I stayed with him until he fell asleep. I told the nurses to call me if anything changed. I drove home and went to bed.

The next day I got calls from my sister and Dad's wife telling me about the party and how I SHOULD have been there. I told them what happened with my dad. They asked me why I didn't call them. I told them there was nothing they could have done. They seemed OK with that decision. We ended up moving my dad to a nursing home. He was ninety-four, and he was not doing well or eating much. At first he knew where he was. But what little was left of his health was fading. We then moved him to hospice care. It was just a matter of time before he lost his battle with dysphagia. He died January 11, 2013, in the afternoon. I got the call from my sister and told her I was on my way.

I know that everyone handles grief and loss in their own way. But what happened next blew my mind. I couldn't even make this shit up if I tried. I'm so glad my best friend was sitting right next to me to watch what unfolded. If she hadn't been there, I may have thought I was imagining things.

The first thing that happened when I got there was them asking me if I wanted to see my dad. I said no because I had seen him at eight thirty that morning. He was sleeping and his breathing was shallow. I kissed him on his forehead and said good-bye. My sister kept saying she was so glad to be there with Dad's wife when the nurse told them to go into my dad's room, that he was taking his last breaths.

My stepmother's kids who lived in town started arriving. My sister's best friend arrived. I called my aunt and cousin to let them know. I called the Rabbi's office to let him know. Then the insanity began. My stepbrother started talking as if he were going to make decisions about the service. Then he stopped and said, "Well, I guess that's really up to the daughters." I remember thinking, you think? Next he called the other stepbrothers that lived in Los Angeles, as did a couple of his kids. He put them on speakerphone. I was sure the people in Los Angeles were going to say we're sorry for your loss or something appropriate. Instead they asked when the service was going to be. We told them Monday, January 14. The next statement will blow your mind. One of the brothers said, "Can't you wait until Wednesday when we can get a cheaper fare?"

My vision went blurry; my ears started to ring. My best friend grabbed on to my hand and squeezed it tight. I looked at her. Telepathically we had an entire conversation. They hung up the phone, and the next thing I knew, my dad's wife started barking orders at me. "You have to call the synagogue! You have to make the arrangements!" Ah, I'm "the help" once again, not a member of the immediate grieving family…"the help." Wow. Mind you, none of these orders were being barked at my sister. In fact, my sister said to me later that day, "I don't know why she didn't ask me to call the caterer. I've done it before." The next day I got a call from my dad's wife's best friend, and she said she was going to take care of all of the catering stuff. I thanked her.

Saturday morning we all met at the funeral home. I barely said a word. All the arrangements were made, and I was glad to go home. Sunday we met with the Rabbi at the synagogue. We were all sitting in this big conference room. There were four conference tables pushed together. I found it interesting where we wanted to sit.

In the furthest corner from the entry were my stepmother and stepbrother. In another corner were my sister and her two kids. In the corner closest to the door were the Rabbi, my best friend, and myself. It struck me we were sort of seated as adversaries. It was kind of funny, in a weird way. Again, I was so glad my best friend was there. Let the dysfunction begin!

The Rabbi encouraged all of us to tell stories about my dad. Believe me, there were a lot to tell. Mine, however, had to be carefully chosen. I had written a eulogy for my dad years before. Of course I didn't write it about any specific date or time. I just knew I had to write down the thoughts I was having eulogy-wise. The thoughts would wake me up at four in the morning. I was afraid I wouldn't remember anything I wanted to say if I didn't write them down. In fact, I had told my sister about it, and she asked me to send it to her because, "It would really be too bad if the eulogy was more about you than about Dad." Wow! Anyhow, I digress. Before we started telling our stories, the Rabbi asked if anyone wanted to speak at the funeral. I told him I did. My dad's wife blurted out, "Oh, no you won't! I heard what you were like at your mother's funeral!" I felt myself sit up really straight and lean forward. The next thing I felt was my best friend's hand on my back. I think she thought I may have been pre-paring to go up and over the table at my dad's wife. The Rabbi gave me a quick, surprised glance. I took a breath. You could hear a pin drop in that room. I turned to the Rabbi and repeated, "I would like to speak at the service." Again, my ears were ringing. We took turns telling stories about my dad. The stories my niece and nephew told were emblematic of a man I never knew. I was stunned how much they loved him, how much he loved them. I was glad they had good memories. Someone SHOULD.

After we were done, I met with the Rabbi in his study. He and I had become good friends over the years. I had talked to him about what a bully my dad's wife was before that day. He said, "She bullied you in front of me!" He couldn't believe it. I cried a little. We talked over a few things, then I left.

The day of the service arrived. My best friend was again right by my side. We all met in the "family" room at the synagogue. I don't remember talking to many people. Frankly, I just wanted to get the pomp and circumstance over with. The man from the funeral home was in charge. He lined us all up to walk into the sanctuary. We were seated in the pews, and the music started. A few prayers were said, and the Rabbi called me up to give the eulogy. I had asked him to put his hand on my back if I started to shake. I knew that the service was being recorded, both sound and video. I was very calm. I looked up from the podium, and there were a lot of people there. I noticed two of my friends sitting on opposite sides of the sanctuary. I remember thinking, too bad they didn't see each other when they came in. I looked at my best friend. She nodded and gave me a sly smile. I started the eulogy. Somewhere in the middle of it, I looked over at my sister, and she was grinning like a Cheshire cat. Odd, I thought. My dad's wife was staring at me. I couldn't tell what her expression was. I got done, turned around, and hugged the Rabbi. I quietly whispered in his ear in a sing-song way, "Nah, nah, nah, nah, nah, nah." Of course referring to the "oh no you won't" by my dad's wife said the day before. I went back to my seat and felt nothing but relief. A friend of my dad's presented my dad's wife with a folded flag, being they were both members of the Jewish Veteran's organization. It was quite touching. The grand send off for my dad was performed by a pretty well-known singer who stood up and sang Frank Sinatra's "My Way." It was perfect! Because my dad wanted to be cremated, there was no graveside service. We had planned that for spring.

We adjourned downstairs to a social room, had a light lunch, and talked to everyone. All of this was almost over. Usually Shiva is one week long. My dad didn't want that. So we planned it for one night—that night at the synagogue. My best friend and I went back to my house. We had to be back around six. The last part of the worst of it…so I thought.

My dad's wife decided my sister, and I had to come over to the condo for the next two days to go through all of my dad's stuff. There was so much crap to sort through! Old bills, old files, work stuff, stuff that was his and my mom's. There was an old Xerox machine that he insisted on keeping, books, tons of papers, birth certificates for himself and my mom, all stuffed in boxes, in drawers, and on shelves. It seemed endless. At one time during this cleaning, my sister and Dad's wife ended up in the kitchen together. They were speaking quietly to each other. I walked by just in time to hear my dad's wife say, "You know, your sister isn't going to be happy with the will." *Oy!* What now? What did he do? He had already transferred the extra plot next to my mother at the cemetery into my name. Since he was being cremated, he wouldn't need it. He wanted his ashes in with my mother's grave. So that couldn't be it. I stopped at the kitchen doorway and said, "Why won't I be happy about the will?" She started to stammer, looked at my sister, and said, "Boy, does she have good ears." My sister turned to me and said, "It really won't matter." Once again my father had confided something to her about me. My heart sank.

I made an appointment with the executor of the will to find out what I didn't know. Until then, we kept digging through all of his stuff. I was mad, I felt sick, and most of all I felt alone. What had he done? I found his bank full of change, put all the coins in a bag, and announced I was taking them. He really didn't have much stuff of value. I found a pair of gold cufflinks I had bought him for Father's Day when I was in my twenties. I took those with me too. Again, what had he done? How do I prepare myself? I knew it was going to be bad.

Two days later, I was in the executor's office. I brought my accountant with me (who is also a dear friend). The executor handed me the will. It was mostly the usual legalese until it came to mentioning me. I was in an entirely separate section from my sister. To paraphrase, it said that I was to get no money until I was fifty-five. The executor had the power to grant or deny any request I might make to draw on that money. It would be the executor's discretion whether he deemed my reasons for wanting any money legitimate or necessary. To be honest, I knew when I was in my teens my dad set the will up so I couldn't have any money until I was thirty-one. I never knew he had changed it, but my sister did. She told me he called and asked her if he should change it. Going on with what else was said in this separate section, it basically portrayed me as being of diminished capacity. I could barely breathe. I asked the executor what else I didn't know. I told him this wasn't about money for me. His answer, "Everything's about money and sex." I had to control myself. He was in charge of whatever or however much money this was. As far as I knew, my ninety-four-year-old father had outlived his money, and I was right. There were several insurance policies, including one that my mom was beneficiary. She had been dead for eighteen years at that point. So this would now include finding a death certificate for my mom, which I found in a box of papers the day before. What made this even more insane, it wasn't even a significant amount of money. I was portrayed and treated so badly for what? This? It was enough to pay the next year's estimated taxes, buy myself a Galaxy Tablet, and move from the awful place I was living. When it was all said and done, the executor decided to release all funds to me because I had turned fifty-four in December, and it was now April. I was devastated by the wording in the will. It cut me off at the knees. I cried for months. Who did my dad think I was? Why didn't he want to know me? I, obviously, was just "the help."

While all this mess was going on, my dad's wife/widow was continuing to call and bully me. Her manipulations weren't working anymore. I was saying no to her emphatically. She had called my aunt in Chicago and said something unflattering about me. A switch flipped for me that day. I had had enough! I called my dad's wife and for lack of a better term, "broke up" with her in April 2013. I told her I was glad she made my dad happy. But to me she was nothing more than a manipulative bully. She said, "No one has ever called me a bully before." The smart-ass part of me thought, well, someone evidently had called her manipulative before. She was stunned. I told her I owed her nothing. But I wasn't going to be treated like "the help" anymore—that she had her own biological children who could cater to her. I told her I didn't want to communicate with her anymore. She said, "Well, if you don't want a family." I countered with, "Don't you understand? I never had one." And she said, "Well, OK," and hung up. I hadn't spoken to her since then until I ran into her at a local Target store. I was cordial, asked how she was, listened, and then said I had to go. That was February 2014. I haven't seen or spoken to her since. It does feel like a huge burden has been lifted off my shoulders. I finally feel like I have some peace of mind.

In July 2014 there was an event at the synagogue for my friend the Rabbi. It was his twenty-fifth anniversary of being in the

Rabbinate. One of my stepbrothers is also friends with him. I was pretty sure we'd run into each other. I was prepared. The service was lovely, as was the dinner afterward. I saw my stepbrother from across the room. I started talking to some people, and when I turned around, there he was. Now keep in mind, not one of these step-people called after my father died. After seventeen years of being in the "same family" (I use that term loosely), not one sent a card or called. Not that I expected them to. But I would have loved to have been pleasantly surprised. So what did my stepbrother say to me after a year and four months of not seeing me? "Roberta Brown." Yep, that's all he came up with. I said, "Yes." He started to say something to me, but something/somebody "shiny" went by, and he walked away talking to them. I just had to laugh. I stayed for dinner and to watch the Rabbi play in his band, took some pictures, and left. I got home and called my best friend. I told her what happened. She said, "That's all he came up with?" Pretty funny she felt the same way. I have to say that being freed up from any obligation to see any step-people has made me much happier and healthier. No toxic people in my life anymore. What's the new way of saying that? #PurgingPoison

CHAPTER 11

Family of Choice

Let me tell you about my real family, my family of choice. We are bonded to each other, we don't judge each other, and we are there for each other. Isn't that what a true family SHOULD be like?

Tricia: My best friend is who I dedicated this book to. She has been my best friend since we met in our tenth-grade art class. She was sitting by herself, looking so sad. I felt drawn (excuse the pun) to her. I sat down next to her, and we started to talk. It was such a natural thing. We started to spend a lot of time together. We even shared lockers. The first time I slept over at her house, we got into this big bed together. She had a king-sized mattress on the floor. We finally fell asleep after talking a lot. Somewhere in the middle of the night, she had rolled over and wrapped herself around me. She was sound asleep; I was startled and afraid to move. I didn't want to wake her up. But this was a first for me. She eventually rolled over to the other side of the bed. I talked to her about it in the morning. She said, "Yeah, I do that. I'm sorry." I told her no problem. Nothing like that would make any difference to me. She was my best friend. In fact, she was the sister I was supposed to have.

I learned a lot from her and still do. We have been through so much together. Breakups, breakdowns, family problems, boyfriend problems, sharing clothes, sharing shoes, double-dates—you know, all that girlfriend stuff. I didn't think that anything could tear apart our friendship. But I was wrong. We had a terrible falling out over a boy. It was our junior year in high school, and he was someone I dated. He and I had broken up, and she started seeing him. I can tell you there are girl rules. You don't date any of your girlfriend's exes. It's nothing but trouble. I was devastated. I felt betrayed. We didn't speak for nearly a year. I missed her so much, but I was so mad. We finally had a conversation about it. We both decided to let it go. Boys weren't worth losing a best friend. We agreed to that for the rest of our lives.

About twelve years ago we had another falling out. One I knew nothing about, but she definitely wasn't speaking to me. I called, I texted, I tried to talk to her where she worked, but she wasn't going to tell me what it was about. Months went by, and I was lost! She had broken up with her husband, who I was still in contact with but didn't know why she wouldn't speak to me. She had encouraged me not to cut him out of my life. I had broken up with my fiancé not too long before that. Needless to say, we were both miserable and not talking. All I wanted was to understand what I had done or said. Finally four months later I found a birthday present outside my patio door. It was from her. There was a sentimental card attached. In the card she asked me to call her. I did; we cried. We got together, and she told me this whole story about how her ex-husband had told her about these terrible things I had said about her. I asked her why she believed I would do that. She said when she asked herself that same question, she remembered the promise we made to each other about not letting "boys" get in the way of our friendship. We talked everything out, and as if no time had passed, we went on with our best friendship. Even with our two "boy" bumps in the road, our friendship could not be torn apart. We made a fresh start. I don't know what I would've done without her then or now. We both know that listening is key. We don't necessarily need each other to fix what's going on, we just need to be good listeners. We've been through hell and high water together. We agree that sometimes friends feel helpless, especially during a parent's illness and death. We also feel helpless when we see each other in bad relationships. We just have to ride the wave and hold on. She is my most important relationship. It's a healthy, loving, respectful one. Our relationship is fun loving, and we can communicate with no words at all. The way it SHOULD be.

Glenda: Another family of choice is a girlfriend I met in junior high. We were so close. I spent a lot of time at her house. We even played cards with her mom and grandma. I loved being there. Everyone seemed to love each other the way they SHOULD. They enjoyed each other's company. They liked having me around. She and I laughed a lot. We sang together, we were in choir together. We even tried out for the school talent show together. We sang "Top of the World" by the Carpenters and one other song. We didn't get selected to be in the talent show. We were a little disappointed, but that was OK with us. I still have that sheet music. I have the notes we passed in class too. They are still folded up in a football shape. She came over many years ago, and we opened and read them all. She said about herself, "Boy, was I bossy." I said, "Yes, you were. But that was OK with me." I loved her no matter what, and still do. We try to see each other once a month. It doesn't always happen, but we do play catch-up via the phone.

We lost touch during high school. We would see each other in the hall but didn't have any classes together. After high school she moved away for ten years. We reconnected at our ten-year high school reunion.

She is another friend that was meant to be a sister to me. She is wise, sweet, and wonderful. She is someone I trust deeply. I am very lucky to have her in my life.

Ann: Another member of my family of choice is someone I met in high school. In fact, I met her through my best friend. She is my quiet, artist friend—smart, funny, and talented. When we were younger, I learned about her family's culture. They had Ukrainian ancestry. I learned about painting Ukrainian eggs. I loved spending time at her house. Her parents were very nice but extremely proper. My friend was a little more of a free spirit than her parents would have liked. But I think that was true of all of us.

She was really a lifesaver for me. She was the one who sat with me at the clinic when I ended my pregnancy. She had me spend the night at her house and made sure I was OK after the procedure. She really had my back during a very difficult time. That was the year my best friend and I weren't speaking. I don't know what I would have done without her. We even traveled together. We went to Palm Springs and stayed with my parents. We flew into Los Angeles and had to take a prop jet from LA to Palm Springs. I was terrified on that leg of the trip. I was never so glad to land! It was a nice vacation. We sat by the pool, went out to eat, and rode horses on the beach. She was an accomplished, ribbon-winning equestrian. I wish I could have been as confident on my horse as she was on hers. She was such a natural. We try to get together four to five times a year. We are both self-employed, so our work deadlines get in the way. But that doesn't diminish our friendship, we just pick up where we left off the last time we got together or talked. Just how it SHOULD be.

These women and I make it a point to go out for their birthdays. They were all born three weeks apart from each other. So every year I get to turn whatever age it is in

December and welcome them to it in March. It's always a fun get-together. Over the almost forty years we've known each other, we've realized no one wants material gifts. We want the gift of time to be together to laugh, to share a meal, and share stories...whatever. We also agree, how much material crap do we need?

Even through my bad relationships, my family problems, my agoraphobia, and anxiety disorder, these three women have been rocks for me. July 13 to 15, 2014, I took my first vacation in almost twenty years. Tricia and I drove up to Glenda's lake home. I couldn't believe I was considering it, let alone driving two and a half hours away from everything familiar and comfortable. With all of their support and no pressure, I drove 145 miles away from my home. What an accomplishment! My best friend is the best copilot there is. She knows just how much information to give me and how to deliver it. She read the directions while I drove. I can honestly say I only had a couple bouts of temporary anxiety. My therapist has always told me there's a thin line between anxiety and excitement. Both are adrenaline based. So I just remembered that while I drove. I even texted him when we stopped for breakfast. He texted back, "Congratulations. Now you can plan your trip to California." To which I replied, "One trip at a time, please."

I called Glenda from the road to let her know where we were. Oddly, there was no answer. I figured because she's really not a morning person, she was sleeping. Tricia and I are the "crack of cock-a-doodle-doo" girls. We stopped for breakfast and after we ate I called again. No answer. Strange. I left a message for her. When we got back in the car, she called back. She apologized. She saw that she missed five calls, not all were mine. She said she had her music up really loud and was singing and didn't hear her phone. I told her I had just said, "Well, this will suck if we get there and she's not there." Of course causing Tricia and me to laugh. She laughed too. She asked me where we were. I said in Onamia, about twenty-five miles from Garrison. She said, "Oh, good. I'll see you in about an hour or so. I'm so excited, you're almost here." We kept driving. When we arrived at the lake home, there was some crying, then some squealing, then some laughing. My girls, my family of choice, were so proud of me.

After the squealing, we went outside and took pictures on the beach. We were about ten to fifteen steps from Pelican Lake. It, of course, was the coldest July weekend on record. So much for bathing suits, Jet Skis, and boating. The water was rough, the wind was whipping, and clouds were rolling in. We still sat outside for an hour. When we came back in, Glenda said she had a confession to make. She wanted us to know she was not at the lake home when we called. She had been up until 3:00 a.m. working at her house. She went to bed and set her alarm for seven but slept through it and woke up at nine. When I called from Onamia, she was in her car, listening to music and singing and didn't hear her phone. She was in Garrison, about a half hour ahead of us. She said she didn't want to tell me because she thought I had enough to think about just getting to the lake home. She didn't want me to worry. That was so smart! However, had she told me, I would have asked her to join us for breakfast and we could have "caravanned" to her lake home, but I'm glad I didn't know she wasn't there. Whew!

Those three women are the "core group" of my family of choice. But there are others.

Sharon: My neighbor from twenty years ago. We spent a lot of time together. We bonded over our furry family members. She had a husky that I fell in love with. She would let the husky out into the hallway, and the dog would walk down to my condo and hang out with me...and my cats. Sharon learned how to love cats by meeting my domestic shorthair. He really was much more like a dog than a cat.

But he was the nicest cat I've ever had. He was protective, like a "watch cat."

I've moved a couple of times, and we've never lost touch. We've had some pretty heavy differences over the years, but it's never stopped us from being friends. As we get older, our bond gets stronger. I couldn't ask for someone to be more in my corner at this stage in my life. She worries about dementia due to her family history, and I've promised to visit her in "the home" and reintroduce myself on a daily basis. She calls me a smart-ass and laughs.

Elaine: Another family of choice I kiddingly call "Jesus." She is the most level-headed woman, so together. She's kind, reliable, honest…wait, I'm making her out to sound like a girl scout (or a German shepherd). She's not. But she would do anything to help her friends. I met her at the bank I had my account at. If she knew I was having financial trouble, she would sneak deposits into my account. I asked her not to, but she did it anyway. That stinker! I loved her for that and so many other reasons. I love her for including me at her family dinners. I've spent two Thanksgivings with her family. It's such a warm and lovely place to be. So unlike all my "family" get-togethers. My favorite gatherings were all the Christmas Eves I was included in. I called myself their "token Jew." Funniest part of the whole thing, I knew more Christmas carols than they did! All those years in choir paid off for something. It was like a *Saturday Night Live* sketch.

Beth: She's my funniest friend who can make me laugh no matter what. We met when I was a manicurist. She came into the salon I was working in and heard me talking about a local concert I wanted to go to, but the tickets were sold out. She said to me, "My husband and I have two extra tickets. Do you want to go with us?" And so a friendship was formed. We've been through so much together. We are no longer married to "those husbands" anymore. Our goal, as I see it, is to find the absurdity in life and make fun of it. We laugh, we cry, and most importantly, we support each other.

Leah: Another friend gave me the opportunity to be a "big sister." We met in the underground garage at an apartment building we lived at. We instantly bonded. She is a lot younger than I am. She was having family problems and confided in me. For the first time, all of my family issues came in handy. I felt very much like a big sister to her. We talked a lot about our families. It felt great to bond with her and be helpful to her. I should add, she's a great support to me, as well. I'm very lucky to have met her.

Sharon R: And last, but certainly not least, is the friend I call my "Medical Mama." She and I call each other when we have odd girly medical things happening, like menopausal symptoms. We share so much information and detail that we laugh until we cry. She has helped me understand so many things I'm going through. Even though we don't necessarily agree politically, we are strong supporters of each other. I would be there for her in a heartbeat, as she would be there for me.

I don't need tons of friends. I don't need friends on the periphery. Most importantly, I don't need the world to love me. All I really need is a strong support system—people who are good listeners and people who are good talkers. I am lucky to call these women my "Family of Choice."

CHAPTER 12

"Aha Moments"
Movies, Books, Magazine
Articles, and Conversations

I've always been fascinated by autobiographies and biographies. I think it's because I like to see what people have been through to get to where they are today. In most of those books the writers have had one thing in common—resilience. If you ask my friends, they would agree I have that quality as well. My therapist would say the same. I've even said, "I'm so sick of sticking my hand in the resiliency bucket I could throw up."

I've been lucky enough to have the same therapist on and off for the last thirty-one years. That's a really long time not to be able to bullshit your way through anything. Not that I would even try. I trust him implicitly. Just a few weeks ago I was telling him that at age twenty-one I was planning on killing myself. Everything just seemed to be too much for me. So I went to the Humane Society to say good-bye to the animals, and then I was going to slam my car into a bridge. Guess what! A small, lonely kitten grabbed onto my ankle and wouldn't let go. No matter what I did, she wouldn't let me go. I ended up adopting that five-week-old runt of a kitten. I walked out of the Humane Society with a new purpose—to save the life of a lonely kitten. I can tell you for sure, she saved my life. She became my focus. I named her Brittany (for the actress Morgan Brittany), and off we set on a life together. I took her everywhere. When I was sad and would cry, she would lay across my neck and purr until I stopped crying. She played fetch like a dog would. She would meet me at the door when I came home from work. She was everything to me. She lived to be twenty-five. What a hard, sad day when she died. I will be forever grateful to and for her.

Since then I have rescued many cats. They are my life's blood, my family, my unconditional love. After telling my therapist that story, I asked him why he thought I didn't kill myself. He said, "You're just too damned stubborn." Well, that may be it in a nutshell. He equated stubbornness with resiliency. We then went on to talk about what sort of people have that quality, and luckily I'm one of them.

Let's get back to autobiographies. I knew I had a story to tell, but the anxiety of seeing it in black and white seemed so daunting. I had started writing years ago about my dating experiences after my divorce in 1994. It was really funny stuff. In fact, I may resurrect that book as comedy relief after finishing this book. I thought it would be a best-seller. I'd write and then put it away for long periods of time, probably because I was dating sporadically. Then after an epiphany when I was fifty-one, I realized THE SHOULDING was the book I needed to write. I needed to write my truth, my not-so-funny truth. The epiphany showed me why so many sad, scary, and strange things happened in my life. I am happily single now and able to focus on what's important: healing and telling my story.

There have been several movies that have played a big part in looking at my own life. Tyler Perry movies have been the biggest inspirations. I have spent a lifetime honing being funny to cope with the pain of my upbringing and subsequent relationships. Bad choices come from not knowing any better. If only I would have known about hot grits and an iron skillet (Tyler Perry's *Family Reunion*).

As Maya Angelou said, "When you know better, you do better." That's a lesson not easily learned. She also said, "When someone shows you who they really are, believe them." As simple as that sounds, why is that so hard? I know that in my past I have given too many chances to people, whether they're family or relationships. The relationships include friendships as well as boyfriends. When I started letting those lessons of Maya Angelou sink in, things began to shift for me, a little bit at first, more so later.

My then husband and I joined a different synagogue than my parents. We were at Rosh Hashanah services, and the sermon the Rabbi was giving was about when life begins, abortion, and personhood. He said, "Life may begin at conception, but personhood begins at birth." What an epiphany! I realized I could forgive myself for the abortion I had in high school. We left the synagogue and went right over to my parents' house. At sixteen, I was too afraid of what they would do to me if they knew I was pregnant. I had kept this deep, dark secret from them for years. It was time to tell them and unburden myself of that secret. The oddest thing happened. My mother asked me who the "daddy" was. If she would have stopped and thought about it, it could have only been one person. Before I could answer, my father said, "It's none of your business." Wow! Not what I expected at all. But it was a giant weight lifted off my twenty-eight-year-old shoulders.

I have spent a lifetime trying to learn about myself. I've been in therapy; I've read a lot of psychology books. I've watched self-help seminars and TV shows. One of the most helpful was an Oprah show in the late eighties and early nineties. I think it was John Bradshaw. He was talking about taking your inner child by the hand and walking her/him away from the pain of growing up in a dysfunctional home. What a wonderful exercise! So I visualized taking my young self by the hand and walking down the hill from the cul-de-sac we lived on. For all the times I was told to go play on the highway near our house, I visualized taking my inner child down the road that led to the highway to remind my inner child it was not safe to play on the highway and not fair or nice to be told to go play on the highway. That was twenty-plus years ago, and I remember it as clearly as yesterday. I cried a big cleansing cry.

Oprah's Master Class:

I have learned so much from watching *Oprah's Master Class*. Understanding where people come from and their journey to their present life touches me deeply. The same way autobiographies do. I think I could teach people something in a master class like that. In fact, I'm hoping that's what this book does by telling my story.

The episodes that touched me the most were Cicely Tyson, Stevie Nicks, and especially Lionel Richie. They were amazing stories of struggle and resiliency. There's that theme again.

Tyler Perry's movies have really struck a chord with me. Each movie I've watched, I've taken some kind of lesson from it.

> *Diary of a Mad Black Woman*: Strength and Resiliency (there it is again).
> *Family Reunion*: Things are not always what they seem!
> *For Colored Girls*: Pain and Struggle SHOULD unite people.
> *Why Did I get Married?*: Cruelty is not acceptable.
> *I Can Do Bad All By Myself*: Have faith and believe in yourself.
> *Good Deeds*: You have to live your own authentic life.

When I watch Tyler Perry's movies, they resonate with me. The way he writes his characters feel authentic to me. They demonstrate how people would like to be treated. All people want is to be validated. I didn't get that growing up. But I have it now.

Iyanla Fix My Life—Iyanla Vanzant:

During one of her shows, Iyanla said something that resonated deep within my soul. "If you're broken, you fill yourself with broken people." Although that doesn't absolve me of some of the choices I've made, it does explain a lot about those choices to me.

APB with Troy Dunn:

Troy specializes in finding lost family members and reunites them with their families. I told myself I wouldn't get involved with this show and its search for missing family members with outcomes both good and bad, but I got totally hooked. It has seemed to open up a can of worms for me. I cry out of joy when families are reunited. I cry bitter tears for family members that are abandoned with no explanation why. All of these tears make me think how nice it would have been to have a functional family. How I would prefer I was speaking with my sister now that our parents are gone. How an explanation or an apology may (or may not) help. But there is no resolution—let me rephrase, the resolution for me is to keep my distance from the toxicity that is my relationship with my sister. Sad but true.

Do you think if I told Troy about my crazy-ass family, he would find me a family I could love and would love me and appreciate me for who I am?

I have read:

> Malcolm Gladwell's *Blink*
> Ted Zeff's *The Highly Sensitive Person*
> John Edwards' *If G-d Were the Sun*
> Claire Weekes' *Hope and Help for Your Nerves*

I've read so many others, I can't even remember the names of them. I was trying to understand what was "wrong" with me. My parents and my sister told me all the time there was something wrong with me. It must be true, right? Meanwhile, my parents told my aunt and uncle in Chicago that I was a difficult child. They told them that I misbehaved and caused trouble all of the time. Of course I didn't find this out until a few years ago. I don't know why they would think I was bad, difficult, stupid, careless, and lazy. I was never any of those things. I certainly had my own ideas and opinions. But as you grow up, isn't that what SHOULD happen? As long as you're not hurting anyone with your personal beliefs, you SHOULD be entitled to those beliefs, right?

As I was contemplating writing my autobiography, I read a review in my local newspaper about a book called *Family Trouble* by Joy Castro. http://www.joycastro.com/FamilyTrouble.htm

It was the story of ten different memoirists telling about the fall-out after writing about their families. Well, that piqued my interest! I think I read *Family Trouble* in one sitting. I found it interesting the different things that upset the memoirist's families. Not the things you would think. The lesson I took from each of those writers was to write your own truth and what other family members think of your story and your truth SHOULDN'T matter. So a month later I started writing my truth.

More Magazine, what a great resource for a lot of things. But my true "Aha moment" came to me while reading an article called "Domestic Violence: A Hidden Cause of Chronic Illness," by Alexis Jetter. This article talked about neurological problems, arthritis, migraines, and other health problems. I have printed out and given a copy of that article to every one of my doctors and caregivers. I've realized that domestic abuse, whether it had been my dad or the boy-friends who had beaten me up, it was and is not my shame to carry. If that article helps my caregivers to understand me better, all the more reason they should read it.

I found my journals from high school 1975 to 1976; interesting reading. Funny, I don't write so differently today. Most interesting was a lot of my journaling was done in Forkner Shorthand. That was a class I took, also called speed writing. I loved it! I was top in my class and even went to a state competition. Well, it's been thirty-eight years since I've read Forkner Shorthand. Surprisingly enough, I could still read some of it. I have to admit I had to go to the library and check out a Forkner Shorthand dictionary to reacquaint myself. I thought of it as a decoder. It was interesting what I was trying to keep secret from my parents in case they had tried to read through my journals. My "Aha moment" rereading my journals was I knew, even back then, my parents couldn't be trusted as far as my well-being was concerned.

What I Know For Sure
(This should be a short chapter)

My life is more like a Tyler Perry movie than Rodgers and Hammerstein.

Minimizing what has happened in my life does not make it OK, less upsetting, or less scary.

Trust your gut. Trust your truth.

A kitten saved my life.

There's a difference between a sense of duty and "SHOULDING."

After being told my whole life that there was something wrong with me, I now know I'm the healthy one. Go figure!

Clichés I hate:

Making lemonade from lemons. Sometimes lemons are just that... lemons.

Play with the cards you're dealt. But sometimes the cards are stacked against you, and you have to play anyway.

I have been thinking about donating my brain to science, like the football players are doing. It would be interesting to find out if I had concussion damage and what role that played in my anxiety disorders.

When injuries flare up, so do memories. Unfortunately, recently I was diagnosed with three bone spurs and a bulging disc in my neck, along with compressed vertebrae. Upon the diagnosis, I flipped into PTSD. All I could see was my dad pounding my head into the floor when I was seventeen. I pulled myself together and left the doctor's office. I called my therapist while I was crying and told him what had happened. We met the next day and talked through the PTSD. I spent the day of the diagnosis crying, and a couple days after that, crying and being angry. I felt damaged, scared, and fragile. I called my friends for support. Everyone stepped up. I started physical therapy. I went in for massage therapy. As I have said, the *More Magazine* article was a great resource for me. So along with emotional support, I now had a team for physical support. I even found some spiritual support. I had now surrounded myself with the right people at the right time.

My parents and sister never knew who I was. Obviously, they didn't want to know.

I've always believed that if you don't learn the lesson the first time, you're destined to repeat whatever it is until you do.

No matter what was happening in my life, humor was my great coping skill. I didn't allow myself to cry much. I must have viewed that as some sort of weakness. But I could self-deprecate and laugh. I also have an offbeat sense of humor. I've always said if I didn't have a sense of humor, I would have blown my fucking head off long ago.

I think all that people want is to be appreciated, valued, and listened to. Unfortunately, I didn't have any of that growing up in my house. I think about the stories I've read about parents having another child to harvest bone marrow or blood to take care of a sick child they already had. I don't view my existence in my "family" much differently than that. I was brought up to serve, to parade out to show what a loving, wonderful family we had, to be seen and not heard, and to take out any frustration, however small. I was told I wasn't good enough, smart enough, or even attractive enough. My parents viewed telling me they would pay for a nose job as taking care of me. How things "looked" to others was most important to them.

Maybe it was naïveté that made me want to trust my parents. Regardless of what was going on, you SHOULD be able to trust your parents, right? Trust and safety go hand in hand. So I SHOULD be safe too. But I wasn't safe…ever. I don't think I understood that. I wanted to trust them. So every time something would happen, I would put it in the back of my mind. I was SHOULDING myself. How I thought things SHOULD be. If wishing could have only made it so.

Once I had a better understanding of what would set everyone off, I would try so hard not to do that. The problem with that, what set everyone off changed daily, so you wouldn't have any scenario to use as a constant. There was no way to stay out of harm's way. It was so frustrating.

I'm sure it's shocking to hear I have trust issues. I trust my closest friends implicitly. But any farther than that, not so much.

I want to believe that people are inherently good. But people keep proving me wrong. At fifty-six, that's OK. I have my closest core group of friends. They accept me for who I am. Those are the people I SHOULD trust. I've worked hard on those relationships. They are the most important people in my life.

You can't be everything to everybody. No matter how hard you try. You need to be true to yourself. That is one of the lessons I had to learn. Another lesson is you can't hold other people to the standard you hold yourself to.

Facing your fears is not a bad thing. With experience SHOULD come the power of knowledge.

This resiliency of mine got me to where I am today. It bonded me to lifelong friendships, which are better than blood relatives.

The most important lesson I've learned: I choose me. Not in a narcissistic way, but in a healthy, empowered way.

I've thought a lot about how to end this book. If I want to continue to be my authentic self, I have to end it three different ways.

What I know for sure:

Schmaltzy ending:

People can tell you they love you, but they may not know how to do that. I was going to let that statement stand alone. But after reading it, I think it gives the people who treated me badly an out, and somehow they won't have to own their behavior.

Soapbox ending:

We need to teach our children and young people differently. We need to teach our boys that it is not OK to lash out violently toward anyone. My father SHOULD have known it was not OK to beat me up. Why he didn't know that, I'm not sure. But he was full of rage.

We need to teach our children about having self-esteem and self-worth. It is not OK to be treated badly or to be beaten up. It is not OK to lash out violently, even if it's what we've learned by living in an abusive, violent atmosphere. I, unfortunately, didn't get the lesson. I thought because my father beat me up and my mother was complicit, it was OK for boyfriends to beat me up as well. How would I have known any differently? But as I wrote earlier, I did make a conscious choice not to have children because I wasn't absolutely sure I'd be able to break the cycle of violence. Hence, thirty-one years of therapy trying to understand who I really am and learning not to be afraid of everything, all of the time.

Smart-ass version:

Costco Kirkland brand paper towels are the best paper towels I've ever used.

ABOUT THE AUTHOR

 Roberta Brown was born and raised in a suburb of Minneapolis, Minnesota. She has always written, whether it was in journals, short stories in writing classes in high school, or business letters with a clever twist. Roberta's obsession with Cher and Cher's nails led her to go to cosmetology school and get her manicuring license. After being in the beauty business for twenty years, an anxiety disorder forced her to change direction. Roberta reinvented herself and started her own business as a marketing consultant and client-services director working from home. That business is small and going strong to this day. *THE SHOULDING A Story of Resilience and Hope* is her first book. Roberta continues to live in the Minneapolis area with her cats, better known as her "fuzzy children."

CPSIA information can be obtained
at www.ICGtesting.com
Printed in the USA
FSHW021316290319
56672FS